All the best from
the Top End,
David Hancock.
2007

Dar Leslie & Marion
Much Love
Monica
x x x

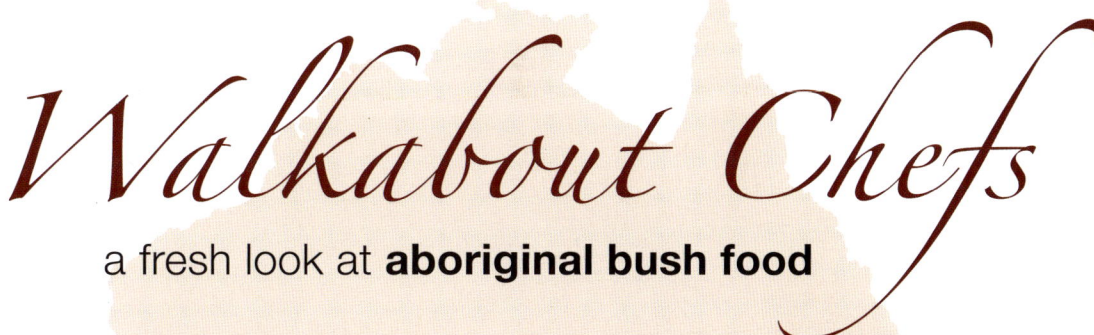

# Walkabout Chefs

## a fresh look at **aboriginal bush food**

by Steve Sunk and David Hancock

Aboriginal people have hunted indigenous plants and animals for thousands of years and continue to do so today. While many native species, such as dugong, turtle, bush turkey, crocodile and even water lilies, are protected under Australian law, Aboriginal people have a legal right to hunt and gather these plants and animals for their own consumption.

The authors recognise these rights and have provided a list of ingredients that can be substituted for protected species. All food shown in **Walkabout Chefs** was caught or gathered by Aboriginal people and cooked under their guidance.

The authors would like to thank those Aboriginal communities and individuals who assisted with this publication – their insight to country and the cycles of life left us in no doubt that indigenous knowledge is one of the most precious Australian commodities. To understand even a little, is of immense benefit in appreciating the continent of Australia and its original inhabitants.

David Hancock

First published in 2006 by SkyScans Australia
GPO Box 2845 Darwin NT 0801 Australia
Telephone: 61 8 8988.4388 Facsimile: 61 8 8988.4344
email: david@skyscans.com

Publishers: SkyScans/David Hancock and Ginette Kenney
Managing Editor: David Hancock
Production/Creative Director: Ginette Kenney
Cuisine Editor: Jackie Fuchs
Proofreading: Brenda Finlayson and David Moody
Layout Consultant: Sue Dibbs
Graphics Consultants: Ulla Conrad and Semko
Printed by Custom Press, 19 East Street, Brompton, SA 5007

The publishers would like to advise Aboriginal people that there may now,
or in the future, be images of deceased people contained in this book.

National Library of Australia Cataloguing-in-Publication data:

Hancock, David, 1954-
Sunk, Steve, 1954-
Walkabout Chefs

Includes index.
ISBN 0-9751800-1-0
1. Aborigines, Australian – Australia, Northern, Central – Food
2. Aborigines, Australian – Australia, Northern, Central – Culture
3. Aborigines, Australian – Australia, Northern, Central – Bushtucker
4. Aborigines, Australian – Australia, Northern, Central – Cookery
I. Title.

641.5929915

A wide cavern in the Arnhem Land escarpment, near Katherine, was home to generations of Jawoyn people. Blackened fire pits mark the entrance while, inside, rocks are smooth from people sitting and socialising; round stones used for grinding seeds into flour are scattered about the cave floor. Directly opposite and to both sides of the cave are rock walls decorated with age-old motifs such as Bolung the rainbow serpent, a creator of life in southern Arnhem Land.

Previous page L to R: whistling ducks; turtle eggs in the sand; file snake; flying fox; water monitor; lily; bush turkey; pignose turtle.

Malcolm Wilson and Mary Martin from Nauiyu community, south-west of Darwin in the Northern Territory, collect water lilies and long-neck turtles at Mission Billabong. The flowers, stems and seeds of the lilies will make a natural bush salad while the turtle, which used to be cooked simply in the coals of a fire, will be part of the new bush tucker cuisine popular at Daly River.

page **contents**

8     Recipes

10     Foreword

13     Introduction

16     Aboriginal Australia map

18     Rhythm and tempo

32     Saltwater

68     Freshwater

110     Desert

148     Bush baking

160     Captions for chapter openers

164     Alternative ingredients

164     Where to buy bush tucker

165     Postscript

166     Project support

168     Acknowledgements

# recipes

**saltwater** dishes
pages 46-59

**freshwater** dishes
pages 82-109

**desert** dishes
pages 128-147

**bushbaking**
pages 152-159

mud crab
omelette

47

stir fry turtle

49

sea turtle
panfried in wild
pepper berry

57

dugong steaks
with bush fruits

59

stingray balls

67

home style
magpie goose

83

chargrilled crocodile
tail with bush
tomato chutney

91

turtle broth

93

panfried magpie
goose breast with a
bush peach glaze

95

turtle liver risotto
with crispy turtle
tripe and pilaf rice

103

freshwater
mussel curry

105

barramundi
with freshwater
prawn bisque
107

bush meat pie with
kangaroo, bush
turkey and emu

133

bush turkey
casserole
135

stuffed bush
turkey leg
roasted
137

witchetty grubs
with pasta
145

bush turkey
breast with bush
tomato chutney
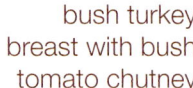
147

bush tomato
scones

153

dugong curry macassan style

51

shellfish salad with turtle egg

53

roast red snapper

55

fish stew

61

grilled crayfish

63

steamed mud mussels

65

smoked crocodile salad with rye berry vinaigrette

85

baked billabong barramundi

87

wild greens and crocodile frittata

89

wattle seed pancakes with sugarbag caramel
97

wallaby saddle with wild plum sweet glaze

99

water lily salad with red claw yabbies

101

fish stock pilaf rice freshwater prawn bisque
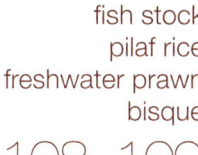
108, 109

kangaroo bourguignon

129

kangaroo tail with pasta

131

kangaroo tail soup with witchetty grubs

139

grilled kangaroo steak with fried bush yam, tomato and mushroom

141

goanna and vegetable stew
143

bush pudding

155

basic bread scratch mix

157

bush muffins

159

## Foreword: food brings us together

**Nauiyu** is a community south-west of Darwin in the Northern Territory. It is located on the beautiful Daly River. There is a rich source and great variety of good bush tucker around the Daly River including barramundi, wild honey (sugar bag), crocodile, turtle, water lily, red claw yabbies, magpie geese and yams, to name a few.

Steve Sunk came to our community to share his gourmet cooking skills with our young people and find out about our local area and the bush tucker. He was given plenty to think about. He took with him new knowledge and a greater understanding of Aboriginal culture in our region.

Everyone, both young and old, enjoyed the trips out bush with Steve. It was another opportunity for the older ladies to share their food gathering knowledge with the young people. Bush tucker gathering is a part of our daily life and from the time our children are able to get around they join in the hunt for bush tucker. Each time the young people go on a bush tucker trip, they increase their knowledge, as the seasons bring different varieties of food. Steve showed us some gourmet cooking tips which were new to us to include in our food preparation.

Through food we discovered a common thread that wove together indigenous and non-indigenous culture.

Steve is well known in many Aboriginal communities in the Northern Territory for his great cooking. I am so pleased that he has written this book as a tribute to the Aboriginal women that he has met during his bush tucker trips. They are remarkable women who have so much experience and were generous in sharing their knowledge with Steve.

Yerr Kinyi ngani tye yerr wirrim ta awa yaga ngan dani wirr fi mi tyatit tye mi bulbul mi nayin werri.

Miriam Rose Bauman
Senior Elder and AM, Nauiyu

Practical lessons start when Aboriginal children are very young. After a hunting trip, Miriam Rose Bauman teaches Nauiyu children about the important spiritual role of the agile wallaby, then describes which parts of the animal are best to eat and how to cook the meat.

Steve Sunk walks through the bush with young cookery students from Wadeye. The two-way exchange of information benefits all parties – the students become better cooks while the chef learns about bush foods and traditional cooking methods.

**Introduction:** journey to another world

# A decade ago I embarked on an incredible journey that led to this book.

Employed by Charles Darwin University and helped by indigenous women, I created the Back to Basics cookery program that aims to improve health, nutrition and employment at Aboriginal communities throughout the Northern Territory.

The Back to Basics program takes cookery to indigenous people instead of bringing them to the city, so they don't feel displaced by leaving their families.

Daly River was the first community to run the program and we had great success. This is also where I got the nickname of Walkabout Chef from two Aboriginal mates, Barak and Ronald, who were the first blokes ever to do a Back to Basics cooking course, along with 12 women.

On average, I deliver the program to ten communities a year, ranging from remote coastal settlements to tiny desert townships. I try to blend European cooking styles and techniques with bush tucker, often turning out exotic dishes like goanna risotto, bandicoot stew, turtle soup and dugong curry.

I do this because it is usually easier for my students to collect bush food than ingredients sourced from a supermarket, where prices are very high due to freight costs.

My solution has been to combine bush foods with everyday items that can be bought from the local store. The idea is to produce economical and tasty dishes by making a stew or hot pot with some vegies and rice, rather than just throwing a wallaby on the coals.

Improving diet is only one part of the Back to Basics program. People also learn new skills and cooking techniques and, by converting recipes into easy forms of measurements using cups and spoons, numeracy and literacy are also improved.

The ladies and I share our knowledge and stories, plus loads of laughter – especially when we go hunting and gathering. The men always laugh and joke because they think I do women's work.

The ladies are great pranksters and, usually, it is me at the end of their mischief – like the time when they threw a king brown snake into my kitchen! They all screamed and I acted scared too. By the way, the king brown was dead!

I have a wonderful time learning from the ladies about their culture and a great time putting dishes together. Occasionally this is met with mixed responses, especially from the older ladies who, bless them, still love roasting everything on the fire.

The most positive outcome from the Back to Basics program — besides improving health and hygiene, mixing culture, increased employment and better family life, is the interaction between the young and older women, and even a few fellas.

## 'Cooking now is no longer women's business'

When I last went out bush, young people took a great interest in learning from the older ladies who were keen to show their skills at gathering food and bush medicine.

We brought our catches to the kitchen where I taught everyone European-style cookery, blending the foods simply but stylishly. At the end of the day we sat down to enjoy our feast with a few stories thrown in and, of course, the old favourite – billy tea and damper.

So the picture is complete.The young are being taught the old ways and learning to blend them with European ways from a white fella to create a great harmony of dishes and cultures.

So far I have trained more than 1,000 students at communities around the Northern Territory and am still going strong. It is extremely rewarding seeing the joy and self-esteem that the students gain by completing the course.

The inspiration to bring these recipes together comes from many ladies that I meet in Aboriginal communities. They are strong women who want only the best for their communities and for future generations.

These recipes give new ideas for foods that have been eaten over many thousands of years, with nutritious options and ways to make special meats go a long way to feed large families. Importantly, the recipes share Aboriginal culture from different regions — the desert, rivers and coast.

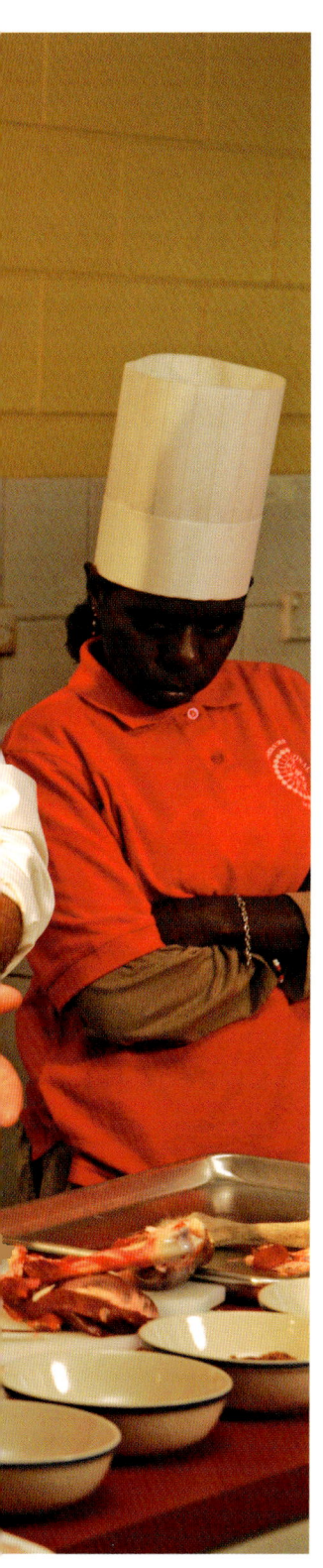

The photography of David Hancock and precise, easy-to-understand editing of Jackie Fuchs have brought these recipes to life. I hope, also, *Walkabout Chefs* will give an insight into Australian indigenous culture and the important role that plants, animals and country play in Aboriginal life.

I hope you enjoy the taste sensations and experiment with your local foods to enjoy what they have to offer.

This book is dedicated to Aboriginal people, especially the women I have worked with. This is their story.

Steve Sunk
Senior Lecturer in Cookery, Charles Darwin University

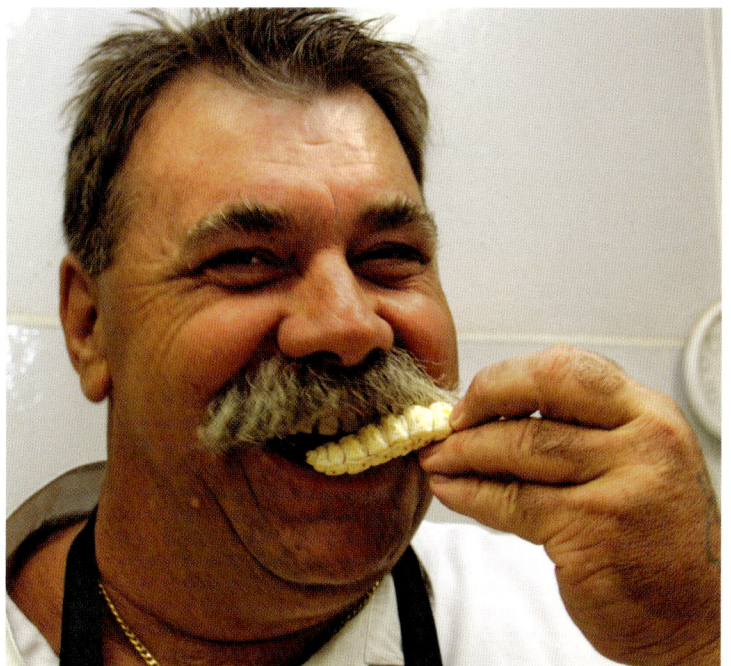

Opposite page: Cookery classes at Wadeye, in northern Australia. L: The chef tastes the ingredients of witchetty grub pasta. Below: Lunchtime at Titjikala in central Australia.

# Aboriginal Australia

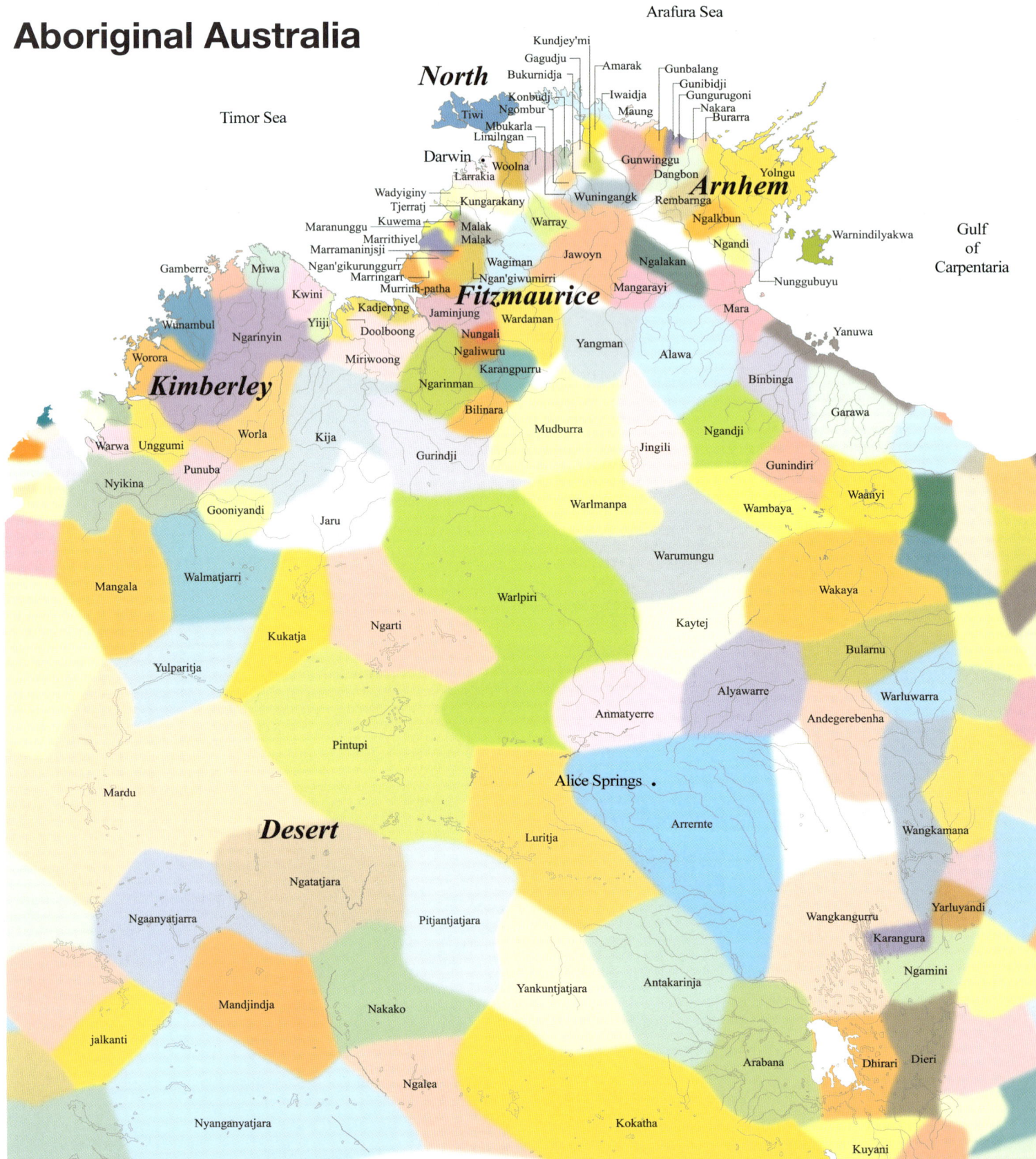

Arafura Sea

*North*

Timor Sea

Kundjey'mi
Gagudju
Bukurnidja
Amarak
Gunbalang
Gunibidji
Iwaidja
Gungurugoni
Maung
Nakara
Burarra
Konbudji
Ngombur
Tiwi
Mbukarla
Limilngan
Gunwinggu
Woolna
Dangbon
*Arnhem*
Yolngu
Darwin
Larrakia
Rembarnga
Wadyiginy
Kungarakany
Ngalkbun
Tjerratj
Warray
Ngandi
Warnindilyakwa
Kuwema
Malak
Malak
Jawoyn
Maranunggu
Wagiman
Ngalakan
Marrithiyel
Ngan'giwumirri
Nunggubuyu
Gulf
of
Carpentaria
Marramaninjsji
*Fitzmaurice*
Mangarayi
Ngan'gikurunggurr
Murrinh-patha
Mara
Marringarr
Yanuwa
Kadjerong
Jaminjung
Wardaman
Yangman
Alawa
Gamberre
Miwa
Doolboong
Nungali
Kwini
Yiiji
Ngaliwuru
Wunambul
Ngarinyin
Miriwoong
Karangpurru
Binbinga
Worora
Ngarinman
Garawa
*Kimberley*
Bilinara
Mudburra
Ngandji
Warwa
Unggumi
Worla
Kija
Gurindji
Jingili
Gunindiri
Punuba
Waanyi
Nyikina
Gooniyandi
Jaru
Warlmanpa
Wambaya
Wakaya
Mangala
Walmatjarri
Warumungu
Kukatja
Ngarti
Warlpiri
Kaytej
Bularnu
Yulparitja
Alyawarre
Warluwarra
Anmatyerre
Andegerebenha
Pintupi
Mardu
Alice Springs
Arrernte
Wangkamana
Luritja
Wangkangurru
Yarluyandi
*Desert*
Ngatatjara
Karangura
Ngaanyatjarra
Pitjantjatjara
Ngamini
Antakarinja
Mandjindja
Nakako
Yankuntjatjara
jalkanti
Arabana
Dhirari
Dieri
Ngalea
Nyanganyatjara
Kokatha
Kuyani

**Aboriginal Australia:** tribal boundaries

# Early European settlers regarded Aboriginal
people as recent arrivals and nomadic, with no attachment to the country they
inhabited. In fact, nothing could be further from the truth. In the early 20th Century,
anthropologists began to confront and change these stereotypes and show that
Aboriginal people had a long and deep relationship with the land and possessed
their own distinct territories.

One of the first tribal maps of Australia was published in 1940 and others that
followed show there were 500-600 tribal groups, speaking many different
languages.

The indigenous people who made up these varied tribal groups had attachments to
the land that date back tens of thousands of years. Excavations at archaeological
sites around Australia confirm that Aboriginal people had adapted to the continent
by developing strategies to cope with a changing environment.

It is believed that up to 300,000 Aboriginal people occupied Australia prior to
European arrival but those numbers dropped to around 80,000 during the 1800s
and 1900s. Now, Aboriginal people make up two per cent of the Australian
population, or around 400,000 people.

In the Northern Territory Aboriginal people comprise around 30 per cent of the
population and own more than half the land, including 80 per cent of the coastline.
The *Federal Land Rights Act* ensures that many tribal groups control their traditional
lands. As a result, many of their customs remain intact, especially those associated
with food gathering.

Today, indigenous knowledge has become highly valued; Aboriginal lands and
coastal waters continue to be a larder for nourishing food and demand is growing
within mainstream Australia for bush tucker.

This map is a section taken from the
Aboriginal Australia map, compiled
by David Horton and published by
the Australian Institute of Aboriginal
and Torres Strait Islander Studies
(AIATSIS). It covers the Northern
Territory and northern part of
Western Australia.

The map indicates only the general
location of larger groupings of
Aboriginal people. Boundaries are
not intended to be exact but give an
idea of the location of tribal groups
mentioned in *Walkabout Chefs*.

The authors would like to thank
AIATSIS and David Horton for
permission to reproduce part of the
Aboriginal Australia map.

'*The changes between seasons of the land are essential for our survival. Knowledge of the billabong, rivers and behaviour of plants and animals at certain times of the year helps us know what bush foods are ready. The 'knock-em down' time (after the wet season) is when speargrass drops and a time to hunt echidna, which are nice and fat. The billabongs are full of turtle, lily bulbs, mussels, prawns and yabbies. In the dry season, also known as burn-off time, the land is black and charred but it helps germinate new growth. The python and goanna sleep and this is the best time to hunt wallaby when they are looking for new grass to eat. When the build-up (to the wet season) comes, it is time for berries and crocodile eggs along the river, and spearing barramundi as they are more active when the water warms up. Then the wet season arrives and the land is alive with colour and new life. Now it's time to face another cycle. We, as people, live the cycle as well.*'

Miriam Rose Bauman
Naiyu Community

*Rhythm and Tempo*

Life for traditional Aboriginal people of northern and central Australia is closely attuned to the rhythm of the land, tempo of the climate and cycles of the natural world … a lifestyle shaped by observing nature and adapting to the environment over thousands of years.

Their view of country is deep and three dimensional, embracing a living landscape influenced by weather, tides, fire and the life cycles of plants and animals. Indigenous Australians look over, under and through this country and see it as few western eyes could.

For non-indigenous people, the north appears to have only two seasons – the wet and the dry. Large thunderstorms, monsoonal downpours, floods and intense

humidity typify the wet season while the dry season is a time of clear, blue skies, cool nights and balmy days. For those who live in the north there are clearly two other seasons – the oppressive build-up to the wet season and the sunny, but moist, post-wet period.

However, Aboriginal people instinctively understand the mystery of seasonal change and can distinguish up to eight seasons, depending on where they live. Unlike a western calendar, the Aboriginal calendar can vary from year to year depending on climatic circumstances – for example, a clear signal of change could be something as simple as a flowering plant, an insect call or the wind blowing from a different direction.

Clockwise from top left: Women from Nganmarriyanga community, south-west of Darwin, use long sticks to search a dried up billabong for turtles buried in the mud; magpie geese and other waterfowl sift through the murky waters of a Top End billabong late in the year when conditions are harshest; hands plucking sweet, green plums (right), holding 'dol dol' or bush cucumber, and cupped around bitter Kakadu plums that are high in vitamin C; a revered sea turtle clan motif is painted on the back of an Aboriginal man at Ramingining, in Arnhem Land.

Over page: On the edge of the Simpson Desert in central Australia, a dune of red sand, colonised by clumps of spinifex grass, is home to many small reptiles; a respected woman from Titjikala, in central Australia, leads the young girls in a ceremonial dance.

Aboriginal people are familiar with the habits of wildlife and regard many native animals as family; some take on totemic importance to particular clans and are never to be eaten. Indigenous Australians know where animals live and hide, which parts of the animal are best to eat and when to hunt the animal in order to preserve the natural balance.

The tempo of the land and the life history of other beings are entwined with the lives of Aboriginal people, who understand that almost every species of edible plant and animal attains peak condition — and that there is a perfect time for harvesting.

Jawoyn and Wagiman people around Katherine, in southern Arnhem Land, recognise that when the bright yellow flowers of the kapok tree are blooming, freshwater crocodiles and turtles are carrying eggs; when the same scrawny tree produces a green bulbous fruit it is time to dig those eggs from the sandy banks of Top End rivers to eat.

The Bining people of western Arnhem Land point to the flowers of the narrow-leafed bloodwood and know that stingrays are fat and ready to be hunted, just as the bright mauve flowers of the turkey bush indicate that shellfish, particularly oysters and mussels, are right to be eaten. When ripe seeds fall from aquatic pandanus trees into rivers and billabongs, freshwater turtles are nearing prime condition.

Traditionally, magpie geese eggs were gathered from sedge and reed nests on the floodplains by northern clan groups such as the Gagudju and Mirrar, who hunted from paperbark rafts at the end of the wet season. Sea turtle eggs are dug from coastal beaches late in the year after females come ashore to lay.

Long-neck turtles, fat from gorging on insects and marine creatures during the luxuriant northern wet, carry good condition into the dry and can be found at the bottom of billabongs or buried under the mud of dried-up waterways, plump and healthy.

In the desert, annual seasonal changes between wet and dry are not as pronounced and the environment is more influenced by prolonged dry spells, or droughts. Aboriginal people have responded to cycles of good and bad years by developing survival strategies that left them fit and healthy even in the leanest years.

Despite the parched, bleak times of drought, the deserts of central Australia contain full larders of food and water. Prospering depends on having the right eye and understanding where to look.

The Arrente, Luritja, Anmatyerre and other desert people know that a flock of zebra finches indicates the presence of water and that a burrowing frog retains significant amounts of water, as does the bush potato, a large tuber with soft, white flesh that can be found near the surface in good times, and deeper in dry times.

Clockwise from top left: The X-ray style of painting that has been popular with Arnhem Land artists for more than 2000 years, details the physiology of a magpie goose at a rock art gallery at Mt Borradaile; a long-neck turtle adorns a gallery in Kakadu National Park; a more recent painting of a flying fox, or fruit bat, at Keep River National Park, in the west of the Northern Territory; a Saratoga fish decorates the underside of Ubirr Rock, Kakadu NP.

The shape of an acacia tree known as the witchetty bush enables water to be funnelled centrally to shallow roots and its fallen leaves form a carpet that helps retain moisture in the soil. While the sands burn, desert people dig the roots that contain fat witchetty grubs, one of central Australia's best sources of protein. Much of life in the Red Centre is underground and much of the food is dug from burrows, logs, trees and roots.

Throughout Australia, Aboriginal people moved around their land to harvest animals and plants and it was no coincidence that when Europeans arrived they found abundant wildlife. Australia, under indigenous stewardship, was an extremely well-managed environment.

In the north, small family groups travelled to the coast to feast on fish and crustaceans and take advantage of waters that flowed hundreds of kilometres carrying nutrients to marine creatures; later they turned to the floodplains, then billabongs and rivers as low-lying areas dried up. They ranged far and wide, often burning areas that would regenerate with fresh grasses, attracting more wildlife.

Plants and animals play a central role in Aboriginal existence and indigenous mythology relates as much to the creation of the natural world as the lives of the

people. Vivid rock art on ceilings and walls of caves and galleries, in which the first Australians lived for centuries, attests to the importance of fauna and flora.

Drawings from about 8000 years ago depict yams, tubers that are rich in carbohydrates and still an extremely important food group today. Paintings in the decorative X-ray style popular in western Arnhem Land about 4000 years ago are so incredibly detailed that many animals – such as catfish, barramundi, magpie geese and crocodiles – can be identified as individual species. Their internal organs and other important features, such as deposits of fat, are shown as if in cutaway – hence the term X-ray art.

Men with spears, clubs and throwing sticks generally hunted birds and animals while women gathered insects, fruit, seeds and tubers. Some foods required extensive preparation such as poisonous seeds from the cycad, a plant commonly found in northern forests and open woodlands. Toxic seeds are chipped and soaked for days before being ground into flour and baked into cakes.

Water lilies are regarded as good 'walking tucker'. Petals can be eaten and the stems are crisp and crunchy like celery; the fruit, or seeds at the centre of the flower pod, are eaten raw or ground into flour and cooked as damper; the tubers or roots are roasted in hot coals.

Shotguns and rifles may have replaced throwing sticks, clubs and spears as hunting implements and four-wheel-drive vehicles replaced long-distance walking, but bush tucker remains the same as it did hundreds, even thousands, of years ago.

Freshwater turtles are prized; water lilies are gathered for snacks; shellfish, mangrove worm, turtle eggs, magpie geese, goanna, fish, fruit and yams are all on the menu today and very much appreciated, especially by older people.

When an indigenous Australian doesn't feel well, a good feed of bush tucker is often a quicker way to better health than pharmaceuticals.

But just as Aboriginal lifestyle has been inexorably altered by western influences, so have eating habits. Community stores are often stocked with fast, heavily processed and refined foods that cost more than they do in the cities because of freight charges.

Once among the fittest people on this planet, many indigenous Australians have contracted western diseases or health problems. Nevertheless, some communities are fighting back by insisting that shops stock vegetables, fruit, pasta and rice. At

some desert stores, cooked kangaroo tail has replaced the ubiquitous carton of hot chips as the most popular takeaway food.

Many Aboriginal communities have welcomed healthy cooking courses designed by teaching institutions such as Charles Darwin University. Community leaders encourage programs that incorporate traditional bush tucker with nourishing western ingredients, diverse cooking styles and the use of modern technology such as microwave and convection ovens, and refrigeration.

Aboriginal people have traditionally eaten simple, healthy fare but some of these new dishes are extraordinary: kangaroo tail soup with witchetty grubs, dugong curry Macassan-style, sea turtle pan-fried in wild pepper berries, shellfish salad with turtle eggs, bush meat pie with kangaroo, bush turkey and emu, water lily salad with red claw yabbies, chargrilled crocodile tail with bush tomato chutney, turtle liver risotto with crispy turtle tripe and pilaf rice … the list goes on.

When you bring that much knowledge to the kitchen, the dinner table overflows with interesting and exotic dishes.

Previous pages: Water lilies are popular with many northern Aboriginal clans – the petals of the flower can be eaten, the stems are crunchy like celery, the pods at the centre of the flower contain peanut-like seeds that are extremely nutritious and the bulbs at the base of the plant are eaten not only by Aboriginal people but by

waterfowl such as magpie geese; just as city kids would carry the groceries in from the supermarket, these young children from Naiyu bring home a freshly-shot wallaby that their parents will cook for dinner.

These pages clockwise from top left: Master chef Steve Sunk discusses

the best way to cook a wallaby with students at Naiyu, on the Daly River; Roselle Frith and her niece Henrietta Robertson fish by a billabong in the Victoria River district of the Northern Territory; a cookery student at Wadeye (Port Keats) community braises wallaby steaks.

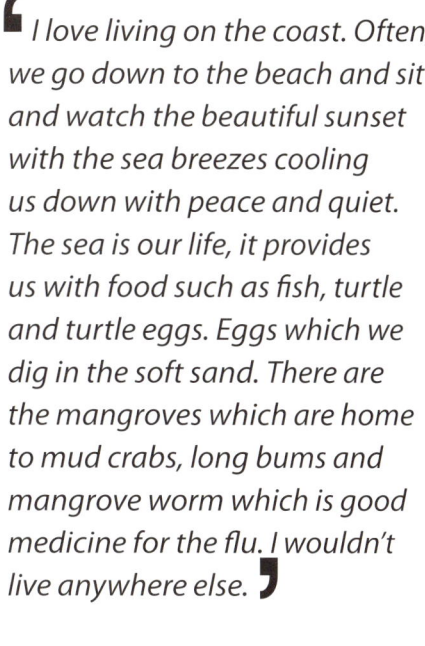

'I love living on the coast. Often, we go down to the beach and sit and watch the beautiful sunset with the sea breezes cooling us down with peace and quiet. The sea is our life, it provides us with food such as fish, turtle and turtle eggs. Eggs which we dig in the soft sand. There are the mangroves which are home to mud crabs, long bums and mangrove worm which is good medicine for the flu. I wouldn't live anywhere else.'

Theodora Narndu,
Wadeye community

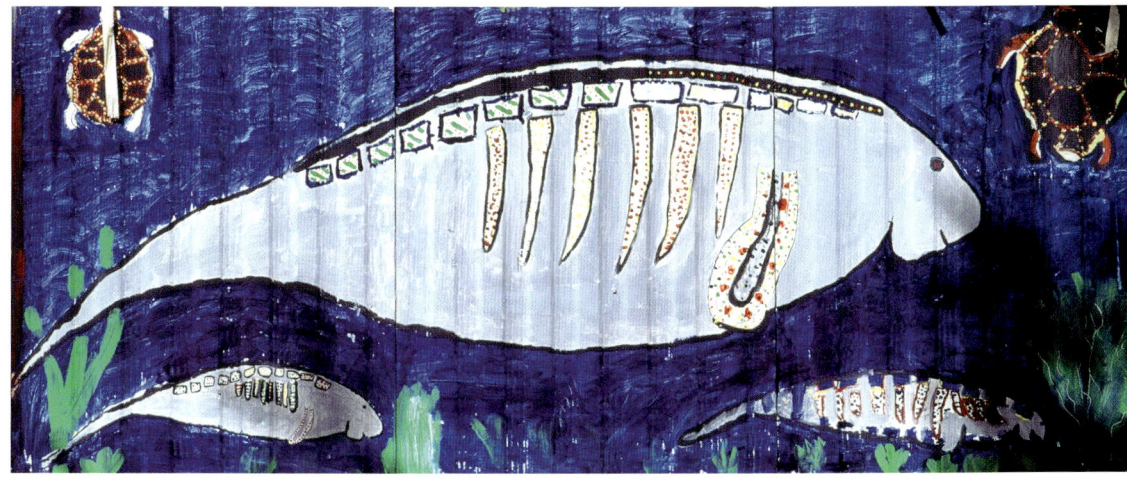

*Saltwater*

Saltwater people have vast resources at their fingertips.

Even though some of their country is underwater, coastal people know the submerged features just as intimately as they know the land – tribal knowledge has built up over generations and dates back thousands of years to times when the landscape was quite different, with lower sea levels and a shoreline that was kilometres further offshore.

Interspersed between hundreds of islands, shallow pastures of lush seagrass attract marine animals like turtles, dugong, dolphins and millions of fish. Tidal variations of up to nine metres expose reefs, mud flats and sand bars to food gatherers searching for delicacies such as mussels, oysters and crabs. Food can be found hundreds of metres offshore on very low tides.

Aboriginal people have waded the shallows of north Australian beaches for thousands of years, harvesting shellfish, crustaceans, sharks, stingray, barracuda, barramundi and other creatures – catching them by hand, in traps or by spear and, in more recent times, with nets and fishing lines.

The rise and fall of the tide dominated the lives of people living on islands and along the coast and they developed sophisticated methods of harvesting the sea's bounty by using the regular ebb and flow.

From the Kimberley coast right around to northern New South Wales, fish traps built from rocks or coral were common, leaving marine creatures stranded in the traps as the tide receded. One highly developed trap, still used by the Larrakia people around Darwin, shows a distinctly Asian influence; it is built from saplings and chicken wire with long 'wings' that direct fish into a central area.

Seafarers from Macassar discovered the rich diversity of northern waters more than 500 years ago when they came to collect trepang, or sea cucumber, popular in Asian cuisine. They, too, explored coastal rockpools and took not only dried trepang back to modern-day Sulawesi but also Yolngu wives from north-east Arnhem Land.

Macassan influence on the local culture was significant – they introduced hundreds of new words to coastal languages, along with important new tools such as the dugout canoe.

The Macassans also left their culinary influence. Along many beaches and coastal inlets grow large, shady tamarind trees that often signal the presence of freshwater springs or wells where the Macassans replenished water supplies. Tamarind fruit has a bitter-sweet taste and can be eaten as it falls or used as flavouring in cooking.

Mudflats and mangrove forests, interspersed with pristine beaches, dominate the northern shoreline. Sea turtles clamber ashore at night to lay their eggs in the warm sand, normally on a rising tide. They lay clutches of about 40 soft-shelled, round eggs that are favoured not only by Aboriginal people but also by marauding goannas and dingoes.

Coastal people such as the Tiwi, Larrakia, Warnindilyakwa and Yanuwa patrol the beaches during laying season, searching for turtle tracks that the tide has not washed away, or for recent disturbances to the sand. They eat the eggs raw or boiled in a billy can or camp oven.

Tamarind trees have become naturalised citizens of Top End flora after being introduced to northern Australia by Macassan fishermen in the 17th and 18th centuries. The trees are found above the high tide mark on many beaches and among the sand dunes; Aboriginal people recorded Macassan visits in their rock art; Asian seafarers ventured to Arnhem Land to collect sea cucumber, which they boiled down in large pots and took home; to this day, Yolngu people of north-east Arnhem Land celebrate their influence by dancing with flags that represent the sails of Macassan praus.

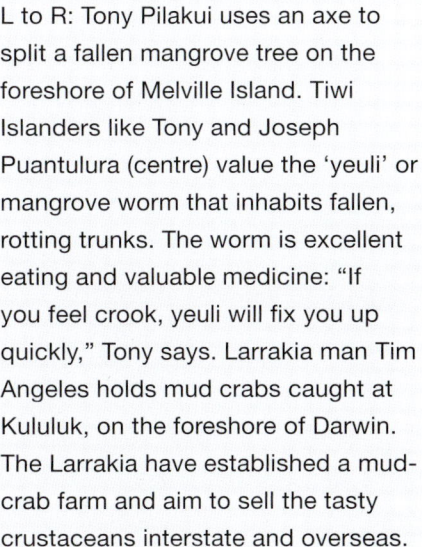

L to R: Tony Pilakui uses an axe to split a fallen mangrove tree on the foreshore of Melville Island. Tiwi Islanders like Tony and Joseph Puantulura (centre) value the 'yeuli' or mangrove worm that inhabits fallen, rotting trunks. The worm is excellent eating and valuable medicine: "If you feel crook, yeuli will fix you up quickly," Tony says. Larrakia man Tim Angeles holds mud crabs caught at Kululuk, on the foreshore of Darwin. The Larrakia have established a mud-crab farm and aim to sell the tasty crustaceans interstate and overseas.

Round turtle eggs resemble ping-pong balls and, once cooked, have a slightly chalky taste; they are much preferred to chicken eggs by coastal people for their nutritional value and health-giving properties. One common claim is that eating the eggs gives a feeling of being 'clear-headed and powerful'.

The mangrove forests of north Australia are among the most pristine in the world. With over thirty species, these plants continue to establish new land by stabilising vast amounts of silt that washes out each wet season. With the assistance of rivers, tidal movement, wave action and even cyclonic uproar, the mangroves colonise areas plant-by-plant until huge forests develop. They are quickly inhabited by all manner of creatures including molluscs, crustaceans, amphibians, birds and reptiles such as crocodiles.

Muddy and often infested with insects, mangroves are one of the best places to look for food. Coastal people step carefully and confidently among the arching buttress roots and between the spiky mangrove shoots looking for mussels and the popular mangrove worm, a long, silky creature that lives in rotting trunks. The mangrove

worm is highly nutritious and is used as medicine; it is common for relatives to bring a mangrove worm and shellfish known as "long bums" into a city hospital to feed sick family members.

Saltwater crocodiles and mud crabs also live among the mangroves. All people wisely avoid crocodiles but mud crabs are a coastal delicacy which range from the beaches and mud flats to deep into the mangrove forests; however, their claws are dangerous weapons capable of taking off a finger or toe. People such as the Larrakia, Iwaidja and Tiwi spear the crabs when they are in the open or place sticks (or wire) in muddy mangrove hollows and pull the crabs out when their claws clamp shut; they then place a foot on the carapace from behind, grasp the nippers and snap them backwards, disabling the crab.

Middens, or prehistoric refuse heaps of bleached shells and animal bones, can be found all along the northern coastline, some up to 100 kilometres inland, providing evidence of how far the coastline has shifted over thousands of years and how long the same food has been present.

The coastal environment changes dramatically throughout the year. December, January and February are peak wet season months and a time when the monsoon drops down from Asia. Heat and humidity are oppressive. Storms and cyclones can batter the coast with violent winds and downpours of rain. Mangroves become refuges for fish and crustaceans that spawn among the roots and in the murky, silt-laden water.

During the wet season, coastal waters turn a cloudy brown colour as floodwaters mix with saltwater; this monsoonal 'flush' extends far out to sea.

L to R: The wet season has arrived and occasionally violent rain storms batter the Top End, churning up the coastline and flushing large amounts of food and debris down the rivers and creeks. Storms may bring chaos but they also provide a time of refreshment, change and plenty; in the dry season the waters of Arnhem Land are clear and tranquil – creatures such as barracuda and stingrays come close to shore and are fair game for Yolngu men and boys who hunt them with pronged fishing spears.

The deadly box jellyfish is a powerful deterrent to swimmers. The jellyfish have delicate tentacles that can trail three metres and inflict severe welts on exposed skin; small children and older people have died from stings. These marine creatures start appearing in October and stay until the cool weather arrives in May. They are hard to spot on a cloudy or overcast day because they are virtually transparent.

In March and April when the rains clear and the floodplains dry out, northern waters begin to settle back to their pristine state. Men and boys take up pronged fishing spears and walk the coast hunting stingrays and baby sharks. Once speared, the long tail of the stingray is clamped between the teeth of the hunter as he knocks out the barb at the base of the tail with a throwing stick or club. Stingray barbs also inflict painful wounds.

As saltwater becomes clear again, large fish such as trevally, queenfish, sharks and barracuda come inshore to feed on small fry, particularly those growing in mangrove nurseries. These fish make a substantial meal for family groups who cook them on coals, or wrap them in paperbark for a more seasoned, steamed dish.

The dry season is a pleasant time for saltwater people: the weather is fine, the water clear and cooler temperatures mean fewer biting insects.

Late in the dry season, springs of fresh water still bubble up on some sandy beaches and it is not uncommon to find soaks of drinkable water only metres from the first sandhill ridge. Large marine animals such as turtles, pilot whales, dugong, dolphins and manta rays gather closer inshore, although dugongs are wary of people.

Coastal people have hunted and eaten dugongs for hundreds of years and scientific studies show the hunting has had little impact on dugong numbers. More dugongs and turtles are caught in commercial fishing nets than are taken by indigenous fishers.

Catching dugong and turtle the traditional way is dangerous work. Once an animal is located at sea by hunters in a motorised dinghy, it is herded into shallow water where a man or boy stands in the bow and dives on its back. To catch a turtle, the hunter endeavours to land with his palm on the shell and grab a flipper to stop the creature from swimming away or diving.

The animal is then hauled into the boat and turned upside down. Turtle and dugong hunters run many risks, as an animal thrashing in the sea can attract deadly crocodiles and tiger sharks. Another risk is being cut by coral when hunting around inshore reefs.

The open waters, sandy beaches, rocky shores, mud flats and mangrove forests of the saltwater country have traditionally provided an incredibly diverse larder for Aboriginal people living on islands or near the coast. Easy access to nutritious, healthy food gave these people time to develop a sophisticated and rich culture that remains largely intact today.

Clockwise from top left: Saltwater ingredients: mud mussels, dugong steaks, prawns and mud crabs.

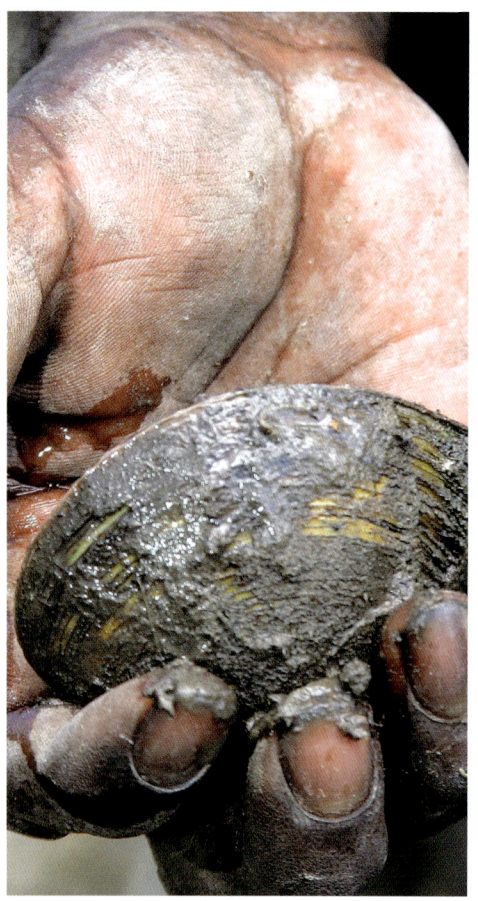

## Mud Mussels and Damper

*On the island of Galiwinku I was teaching a marvellous group of ladies from the community store, women's centre and aged care. The ladies wanted me to take them out to Roger Creek to get mud mussels which live in the black mud flats covered in mangrove and paperbark.*

*We packed up the billy tea, flour, treacle, baking powder and of course, dilly bags for the mussels. Off we went in the Toyota down the track to Roger Creek and set up camp. After a few hours we had our share of mussels. The women used sticks to dig them out. You needed a keen eye. They had 12 mussels to every one of mine and filled their dilly bags quickly. We walked back to camp and made a fire. One of the ladies mixed up a damper and placed it in the hot sand next to the fire, covered it with sand and topped it with hot coals.*

*The other ladies placed their mussels on the hot coals and cooked them till they opened. We shared them around. I tried to pick one out with my hands and, sure enough, burnt my fingers. Next thing, I stood on hot embers which caused me to dance around like I was in a corroboree.*

*The women went into hysterics of laughter. One of them picked up an empty mussel shell which was still joined and sprung the edges together and said, 'Look Chef. Tongs. Use this, no burnt fingers.' We had a good laugh and finished the day with fresh damper, treacle, and billy tea.*

## Preserving Food – Coastal Style

*Another time at Roger Creek on the beach side where the water runs over the rocks and into the sea, the kids were collecting shellfish and the fellas were netting fish ready to put on the fire that was supporting a flour tin of water, boiling for billy tea. The fish were made up of skinnies, cod and a couple of nice-sized snapper. Some fish were filleted while the small ones were placed on the coals.*

*Eventually everything ended up on the coals. This was lunch and there was a hungry mob to feed. I brought along heaps of scones and, of course, treacle which was a good addition to the meat. One of the elders in the community looked after the fish and ensured the fire wasn't going to burn the food. Obviously, with fish, there were a lot of flies around.*

*I asked the elder what they did in the old days when there were no refrigerators to store food. He told me how his ancestors used to move from island to island in their dug-out canoes. They would spear a wallaby. Cut it up, skin and all, and throw the parts on the fire to seal the meat. Once it looked charred, they would wrap it up in paperbark and it would last up to four days. The wallaby would be cooked as it was needed.*

*This is the oldest technique of preserving as the charred areas of the meat would seal the carcass so no air could get to it and no flies were attracted. You learn something new all the time.*

Top left and right: Jolene Killer, Tennille Skinner and Vanita Skeen of Looma community hunting for mud crabs and shellfish on a north Australian beach with Steve Sunk.

Bottom left: Mud mussels are a popular meal in most coastal communities.

*Omelettes are simple and very popular. They can be varied using ingredients such as mushrooms, tomatoes, bush onions, crocodile and frozen or fresh vegetables.*

# Mud Crab Omelette

### Equipment
small camp pan or small nonstick pan
fork
mixing bowl
measuring spoons

### Ingredients
3 eggs or 1 emu egg
salt and pepper
cooked meat from mud crab
(keep in chunky pieces)
1 tablespoon margarine or canola oil

### Method
1. Break eggs into mixing bowl. Season with salt and pepper.

2. Blend eggs with a dinner fork. Do not over beat.

3. Stir in half the crab meat.

4. Heat small camp pan (medium heat). Coat pan with margarine.

5. When the margarine is hot, pour in the egg mix. Shake pan and stir with fork. Let the egg set. Roll cooked egg towards back of pan, letting raw egg slide to the front. When egg sets, roll egg with fork to form an oval shape. remove from heat.

6. Turn omelette onto a plate and add remaining crab meat to top of omelette.

7. Serve with salad or wild spinach.

**Serves 1**

*Turtle meat is a highly prized food source for coastal Aborigines—especially the tripe and liver. The green fat is also eaten. Turtle meat has a very distinctive flavour. Other meats can be used for this recipe like beef, lamb or chicken. These meats are usually marinated.*

# Stir Fry Turtle

### Equipment
camp oven, large heavy frying pan or wok
cook's knife
cutting board
measuring cups
measuring spoons
medium pot
sieve
vegetable peeler
wooden spoon

### Ingredients
2 medium carrots
2 stalks celery
1 red capsicum
1 large onion
4 tablespoons olive/canola oil
2 garlic cloves, crushed
1 tablespoon shredded ginger
3 cups turtle meat sliced into small strips
4 tablespoons each of soy sauce and oyster sauce, mixed in a cup
salt and pepper

### Method
1. Wash, peel and cut vegetables into small strips. Shred onion. Partly cook in boiling water. Strain and set aside.

2. In a camp oven, pan or wok, add oil and heat on maximum setting. Add garlic and ginger. Lightly brown.

3. Add the turtle meat and cook for five minutes.

4. Add the softened vegetables and mixed oyster and soy sauces.

5. Fry for two minutes, stirring constantly.

6. Season with salt and pepper to taste.

7. Serve with rice.

**Serves 4**

*Dugong is only eaten on special occasions. This recipe is a good way for stretching out unique meats. Other options for this curry recipe are chicken or fish. Coconut milk can be used. Cooking time will be one hour for chicken and twenty minutes for fish. Prawn paste, chillies and spices were introduced by the Macassan fishermen. They came to islands like Tiwi and Galiwinku for sea cucumber (trepang) and to take the women as their wives. The coastal Aboriginal people like the hot chilli unlike the people from the desert and rivers.*

# Dugong Curry Macassan Style

### Equipment

bowls
camp oven or heavy pot
cook's knife
cutting board
juicer
measuring cups
measuring spoons
wooden spoon
vegetable peeler

### Ingredients

2 tablespoons olive/canola oil
2 medium onions, finely chopped
4 garlic cloves, crushed
1 thin slice blachan (prawn paste)
6 cups dugong meat, diced small (rib or belly meat)
4 tablespoons curry powder
2 tins peeled tomatoes, chopped with juice
6 whole red or green long chillies
6 medium bush yams or potatoes, cut into bite-sized pieces
salt and pepper
juice of 2 limes

### Method

1. Heat oil in camp oven or heavy pot. Fry onions, garlic and blachan until light brown.

2. Add dugong meat and fry. Stir with wooden spoon.

3. Add curry powder and mix well with the dugong. Add tomatoes and chillies and enough water to just cover the dugong meat. Bring to the boil.

4. Skim top of the pan for any scum or impurities (blood or bone) and simmer for one hour (slow cook). Add liquid when needed.

5. Add bush yams or potatoes and cook until tender.

6. Season with salt, pepper and lime juice.

7. Serve with rice.

### Serves 4

*Mud mussels are found in the mangrove forests. The women look for small cracks in the mud and use a stick to dig out the mussels. Long bums, a cone shaped shellfish, are also found in or on the mangrove mud. Cockles are dug out of the sand on low tide. A favourite food of the Galiwinku women is the salty mangrove worm. The ladies split the rotten mangrove trees and pull out the worm which can grow to one metre long. The worms are generally eaten raw. Mud is sucked from the worm and discarded before eating. Mangrove worm is prized and is used as currency in some communities, especially for card games.*

# Shellfish Salad with Turtle Egg

### Equipment
colander
cook's knife
cutting board
large basin

### Ingredients
1 lettuce, washed, drained and torn into bite sized pieces
12 longbums, boiled and meat taken out
12 mud mussels, cooked meat
24–36 cockles, cooked meat
9 mangrove worms, sand and mud removed then washed
2 tomatoes, cut in thin wedges
1 cucumber, thinly sliced
1 quantity of home made mayonnaise
9 turtle eggs, boiled and shell removed
6 lemon wedges

### Method
1. Place lettuce, all seafood, tomatoes and cucumber into basin and gently mix.

2. Place equal amounts on each plate and drizzle with home made mayonnaise. Serve with lemon and three turtle eggs per plate.

Eggs are harvested from saltwater turtles on coastal beaches and have a very strong flavour. The turtle eggs stay soft when boiled and the texture is very different from other eggs.

## Homemade Mayonnaise

### Equipment
bowl
measuring cups
measuring spoons
whisk

### Ingredients
2 (chicken) egg yolks
1 turtle egg yolk
1 teaspoon French mustard
1 tablespoon white wine vinegar
2 cups olive or canola oil
salt and pepper

### Method
1. Place all egg yolks, mustard and vinegar in a bowl.

2. Whisk yolk mixture until fluffy. Use hand beater if a whisk is not available.

3. Slowly add oil while whisking. Mixture should be thick and white in colour. It should take two cups of oil. If mayonnaise is too thick, add a raw turtle egg or water to the mixture to thin it down.

4. Season with salt and pepper.

**Serves 3**

*This is a nice meal for the family and can be accompanied with cooked rice or boiled yams. The vegetables are cut small due to the short cooking time. This dish is also suitable for wrapping in wet paperbark and placing next to hot coals.*

# Roast Red Snapper

## Equipment
cook's knife
cutting board
grater
measuring cups
measuring spoons
roasting dish or baking tray
wooden skewer

## Ingredients
2 tablespoons olive/canola oil
1 whole snapper, scaled, gutted and washed
salt and pepper
1 carrot
1 red capsicum
1 green capsicum
1 stick celery
1 onion, finely shredded
1 cup shredded ginger
2 garlic cloves, finely chopped
1 cup light soy sauce
1 lemon sliced, skin on

## Method
**1.** Lightly oil fish and cut slits in both sides. Place on a baking tray or roasting dish. Season with salt and pepper.

**2.** Cut carrot, capsicum and celery into matchsticks.

**3.** Mix vegetables, onions, ginger and garlic with soy sauce. Use soy sauce with less salt. Spread the mix inside and on top of the fish.

**4.** Place in hot oven and cook 25 to 30 minutes depending on the size of fish. Check progress with skewer through thickest part of fish. Fish is cooked when skewer comes out clean.

**5.** Serve with rice and garnish with lemon.

**Serves 4**

*This dish was created at the old Garden Point Mission on Melville Island, in the former aged care kitchen. The skirt of the turtle is ideal for this dish which is fast to cook. You can also use fillet steak or chicken breast.*

# Sea Turtle Panfried in Wild Pepper Berry

## Equipment
bowl
camp pan or frying pan
cook's knife
cutting board
juicer
measuring cups
measuring spoons
wooden spoon

## Ingredients
4 hand-sized pieces turtle meat
3 tablespoons olive/canola oil
1 cup native pepper berries or other wild berries
juice from 1 lemon and 1 orange
1 cup water
4 tablespoons lime or lemon marmalade (fruit jam can be used)
1 bunch spring onions, washed and cut into small pieces

## Method
1. Cut turtle meat into flat bite-sized pieces.

2. Heat oil in camp pan or frying pan. Add the turtle meat stirring quickly with a wooden spoon until cooked. Remove meat and place on bowl or plate.

3. In the same pan, add pepper berries and fry until soft.

4. Add lemon and orange juice, and water. Bring to the boil to remove turtle flavours from pan (deglazing).

5. Add the marmalade or jam to help thicken the glaze and give a tangy, peppery taste.

6. Stir in spring onions. Add turtle meat and heat to serving temperature. Do not boil as turtle will become stringy.

7. Serve with steamed rice, mashed wild yams or sweet potato.

**Serves 4**

*The dugong for this recipe can be from the loin or as the picture shows, from the tender rib area. The dugong taste is a bit like heavy beef and can be used in many different styles of cooking such as stewing, braising, frying and roasting. Dugong can be substituted with pork or chicken. The bush fruits help to break down the fatty tissue of the dugong which is highly prized by the islanders. The sauce has a slight acid and sweet taste, like sweet and sour sauce. Honey can be used instead of sugar to take the tartness out of the fruit. Cinnamon sticks can be added to the sauce if available. When the bush fruits are not in season, use ordinary fruit or even dried fruit. Apricots and apples are excellent and complement the dish.*

# Dugong Steaks with Bush Fruits

### Equipment
cook's knife
cutting board
frying pan
measuring cups
wooden spoon

### Ingredients
8 hand-size dugong steaks,
remove excess fat
juice of one lime
1 cup oil
salt and pepper

### Method
1. Rub lime juice onto steaks. Leave for 5 minutes.

2. Heat oil in frying pan. Add dugong steaks and cook until brown. Season with salt and pepper.

3. Place two steaks on a plate and add bush fruit sauce.

## Bush Fruit Sauce

### Equipment
measuring cups
measuring spoons
small pot
wooden spoon

### Ingredients
3 cups wild berries or fruit (bush apples are good to use with plums)
1 cup raw sugar
2 cups water
2 tablespoons cornflour dissolved in 1 cup water

### Method
1. Prepare fruits by removing stones and washing.

2. Place the fruit, sugar and water in a pot. Bring to the boil.

3. Skim off the scum and simmer for 5 minutes or until fruit is soft.

4. Stir cornflour and water mixture, then add to fruit while stirring. This will thicken the sauce.

5. Adjust sauce flavour with extra sugar if desired.

**Serves 4**

*This is a very simple dish and a nice way to cook fish, especially if you catch a few different species. River or fresh water fish can be cooked the same way.*

# Fish Stew

## Equipment
cook's knife
cutting board
camp pan
wooden spoon
measuring cup
mixing bowls

## Ingredients
2 or 3 sea fish (such as snapper)
2 large onions, roughly diced
2 green and 2 red capsicums, diced
2 tomatoes, roughly diced
2 tablespoons olive/canola oil
2 tablespoons sweet red paprika powder
2 cups water or fish stock
salt and pepper

## Method
1. Scale and gut fish. Slice into finger-thick cutlets. Wash and set aside.

2. Wash and prepare onions, capsicum and tomatoes.

3. Heat oil in heavy camp pan. Fry onions until light brown.

4. Add capsicum and paprika. Mix until paprika colours the oil.

5. Add fish pieces, chopped tomatoes and liquid (water or fish stock). Bring to the boil.

6. Remove any impurities by skimming the surface. Cook slowly for 25 minutes, shaking pot every five minutes to keep fish in pieces (using a spoon will turn mixture mushy).

7. Season with salt and pepper. Serve with cooked pasta, Chinese noodles or potatoes.

**Serves 4**

*The local crays around the Top End are known as painted ladies or painted crays. They are a vegetarian type of crustacean, so the best way to catch them is by diving or looking in rock pools on a low tide. If you are diving make sure you take someone along to keep a lookout for those crocodiles. They like crayfish too, and they don't worry about grilling them. Crayfish are sought by the indigenous communities along the coast and Islands. The best way to cook them is to split the cray in half and remove the insides and grill them in their own juices. You can add a few wild berries to complement the flavour, and bush limes or apples are also nice. You cannot beat the flavour of a fresh-caught cray out of water and into the pan; it makes your mouth water!*

# Grilled Crayfish

**Equipment**

cook's knife
cutting board
tongs
pastry brush
griller
rice steamer

**Ingredients**

2 medium lobsters
olive oil or canola oil
½ cup wild bush limes
salt and pepper

**Method**

1. Split the crayfish in half and clean out entrails. Wash meat, lifting it from shell.

2. Place meat back in the shell and brush with liberal amount of oil.

3. Place in a griller and cook until light brown or cooked (8-10 minutes).

4. Chop wild bush limes roughly and sprinkle on top. Season with salt and pepper.

5. Serve with steamed rice.

Note: If a griller is not available, cook over hot coals in the shell.

**Serves 4**

*The elusive mud mussel lurks in the mangrove swamps and is usually collected by the women on the community using a stick to prod the mussel out. You need a keen eye to seek the mussels because the only mark they make is a crack in the mud. The only way to eat the mussel is by steaming over hot coals and eating them straight away, juice and all. They have a fantastic flavour similar to oysters but much saltier. You would think because they live in the mud they would have a muddy taste. This is not so. They are also a great addition to salads, with a mixture of other seafood. This is another precious commodity, like the crayfish, that is best eaten simply.*

# Steamed Mud Mussels

**Equipment**
knives
cutting board
Chinese steamer
tongs

**Ingredients**
24 mud mussels
lemon or lime wedges

**Method**

1. Wash and scrub mud mussels.

2. Place them in Chinese steamer (with steam rising).

3. Cook with lid on until shells open (5-7 minutes).

4. Cool slightly and squeeze with sliced lemon to serve.

**Serves 4**

*Stingray is very popular with the sea people especially on the islands. The old ladies boil the stingray to remove all the meat and pulp it together by hand. They render the stingray fat which comes from the liver and fry the stingray meat until it turns brown. This is a great treat for the family and very healthy.*

# Stingray Balls

### Equipment
cook's knives
cutting board
mixing bowls
wooden spoon
electric blender or wooden club
frying pan or camp pan
paper towel

### Ingredients
2 tablespoons of olive or canola oil
1 onion, chopped
2 teaspoons garlic, chopped
1 teaspoon blachan (shrimp paste)
1 teaspoon chilli, chopped
2 tablespoons coriander fresh or dry
1 stingray or 2kg of meat from flap
2 egg whites
½ cup cream (optional)
salt and pepper
½ cup cornflour or plain flour
2 cups oil

### Method

1. Place oil in a pan and heat. Add onion, garlic and blachan. Fry lightly until onion is clear.

2. Add chilli and coriander. Stir until mixture smells aromatic. Transfer to bowl and cool completely in refrigerator.

3. Remove skin from stingray. Dice meat into small pieces. Place in bowl and pulp with wooden club or use kitchen whiz or blender.

4. Place the pulped stingray into bowl and cool down in refrigerator for 20 minutes.

5. Lightly mix stingray pulp with onion mixture, adding two egg whites and cream (cream is optional but it helps to keep mixture soft). Mix, and season with salt and pepper.

6. Mould mixture into golfball-sized pieces, and roll in cornflour or plain flour.

7. Heat two cups of oil in camp pan. Place stingray balls into hot oil and fry slowly until golden brown. Drain stingray balls on paper towel.

8. Serve with rice, bush limes and sweet chilli sauce.

**Serves 4**

> ' *Living by the river is great because it feeds the community with plenty bush tucker such as barramundi, long and short-neck turtles, water lily bulbs, yabbies and prawns. It is home to salt and fresh water croc and we hunt for their eggs along the river bank. There is great wildlife to see, varieties of birds and animals, magpie geese, wallaby and pigs which we love to hunt and share with the old people. It is very peaceful. There are not too many cars going up and down like a big city and there is plenty of fresh air. People are very close; they all know each other's business.* '

Barak Sam Bono
Naiyu community

*Freshwater*

The freshwater country of northern Australia is bountiful in the extreme.

Almost directly behind the sand dunes of the coast are the Top End's celebrated floodplains that, at the end of the wet season, are among the most productive habitats on earth – a mix of lush grasses and aquatic plants, insects, birds, reptiles and mammals.

Nine months later, at the end of the dry season, a more alien landscape could not be found. Most creatures have retreated from the plains to cooler, greener areas and

dust devils whisk ashes of burned plants skywards from a terrain of parched, cracked soil.

Each wet season, without fail, rivers flood wetlands with nutrients. Unlike other parts of Australia that suffer extended droughts, rain always arrives in the north – the only question is, how much?

Most years, billions of litres of water run off the ancient escarpment country that has been worn back to bare  sandstone over the ages. The Arnhem Land plateau is the

source of scores of rivers that run east, west, north and south. Its surface is gouged deep with crevasses and gorges that house a variety of unique animals and plants.

The stone country is hot and forebidding much of the year but during, and just after, the wet there are pools of water among the rocks and many flowering plants. Later in the year, frogs, small reptiles and rock wallabies seek cool caves and rock shelters. Gagudju, Gunwinggu, Ngalakan and Jawoyn people (and other clans) also sought refuge in these cool, rocky retreats and often walked long distances across the stone country to ceremonial or clan areas.

Then, as now, they gathered sugarbag (honey from non-stinging native bees) from logs or hollows in trees, hunted wallaby and goanna and collected seeds, fruits and yams. People travelling through the bush still suck the nectar from the flowers of grevillea and other plants to boost energy levels.

The rock walls and ceilings of the stone country have been a spectacular canvas for indigenous artists for generations and there are many places where family groups sheltered when lowland areas were hot during the build-up to wet, stormy weather.

Signs of Aboriginal occupation include rock paintings, blackened areas where animals such as wallabies were cooked and smooth rocks where people sat, talked and ate. There are also many grinding stones around the shelters, as well as circular depressions in the rock where plant seeds were ground into flour.

During the wet season waterfalls cascade over escarpments. Some are so full the roar obliterates all other sounds, while others are fine droplets freefalling to the tropical woodland. All this water is channelled into thousands of small creeks that ultimately make their way into some of the largest rivers in northern Australia – the East and South Alligator, Adelaide, Daly and Victoria Rivers. These rivers fill quickly during a big wet, flooding over the banks onto low-lying plains. River creatures like the estuarine crocodile follow fish and other animals out onto the floodplains where they are easy pickings in shallow water.

The floodplains and rivers are a remarkable part of the northern landscape, especially after the wet season. Other habitats such as billabongs, monsoon and paperbark forests remain wet and bountiful for much of the year while the drier tropical woodlands also provide substantial resources for Aboriginal people.

Paperbark forests are usually found in poorly drained areas and are often used by animals and birds as a retreat when the floodplains dry out. Monsoon forests are damp, cool homes to many insects and plants — people look for yams in these areas, as well as ripe fruit during the build-up to the wet season. Yams reveal their presence with long tendrils and leaves that wind around other plants, growing towards the sunlight. The inland people follow "yam strings" back to their source and dig up the tuber. When fruit is not within reach, it is collected after it falls to the forest floor.

L to R: Speargrass is not only a seasonal indicator in northern Australia but its growth can indicate when other plants and animals are ready for harvest; a painting of a large goanna dominates a rock gallery at Umorrduk in western Arnhem Land; an ironwood knife and a piece of steel adapted as a scraper, with resin handles, are remnants from the Contact period when Aboriginal people first came across early settlers in the north of Australia; birds such as this rainbow lorikeet are not the only creatures to enjoy the nectar of a native grevillea. Aboriginal people often sucked on the flowers for energy as they walked.

Clockwise from top left: Plumed whistling ducks enjoy the shade during the heat of the day and fly out at dawn and dusk to feed, their shrill calls and beating wings contributing to the ambience of the wetlands; melaleuca or paperbark trees at Yellow Water in Kakadu NP shelter a multitude of animals, birds and insects and are among the richest habitats in Australia; a large saltwater crocodile lurks in a shallow, weed-covered billabong near the Adelaide River; the Magela floodplain is awash during the wet season as water pours off the Arnhem Land escarpment. Many creatures are left clinging perilously to lower branches of trees as the waters rise.

This page: Large meridian termite mounds are silhouetted against the early morning light during a dry season morning in the Top End of northern Australia; Felina Campion from Maningrida in Arnhem Land holds a tray of saltwater crocodile eggs that will be hatched and sold to farms around the Northern Territory and Queensland – Derrelene Yeeindilli looks on.

Opposite page, top to bottom: Barramundi and saratoga are cooked on the coals as they have been for thousands of years; magpie geese are plucked, gutted and laid over a wire grill to cook over the coals; native yams have played a major role in Aboriginal cookery for thousands of years. Djelk Rangers at Maningrida are cultivating yams in a nursery as part of a bush tucker program.

Floodplains, monsoon and paperbark forests, billabongs and rivers all make up the famous wetland areas of northern Australia and are prime freshwater country. However, the largest habitat is the tropical woodland, or savannah.

This landscape is gently undulating, open and populated by large eucalypts, straggly shrubs and grasses such as native sorghum or speargrass. At a glance, and compared to the rich, bustling wetland areas, the woodland appears to be devoid of life, but nothing could be further from the truth. Many woodland creatures are nocturnal and very good at hiding, like the frill-necked lizard that is dormant in the dry season and active at the start and end of the wet.

A range of creatures - such as goannas, possums, quolls and cockatoos - live in branches and tree trunks that have been hollowed out by termites. The insects have a symbiotic relationship with woodland flora, occupying young trees and bringing nutrients in the form of enriched soil, or nesting material, to the trunk; the termites move on when the tree matures, leaving hollows for animals to inhabit. Aboriginal people search these hollows for game and often use termite-nesting material to

flavour food when it is cooking underground. The material is also burned as an insect repellent.

During the monsoon, wetland areas are hard to access and people hunt around the margins. Vegetation can be submerged for weeks during flooding, leaving branches of large paperbarks and other trees often crowded at water level with hundreds of insects, frogs, goannas and rats. Water pythons enjoy a time of plenty as they swim from tree to tree, consuming stranded mammals.

Barramundi use this time to travel between freshwater and saltwater. Young fish move up the rivers into billabongs where they grow, while adults travel to the sea to breed. Magpie geese feed excitedly on water plants in preparation for the breeding season and aquatic creatures, such as turtles and file snakes, also feed voraciously.

When the rains stop, water levels begin to drop. Anglers look to this time to fish the run-off, as the last fresh water runs from the floodplains into the rivers, bringing tasty morsels to large fish such as the barramundi that patrol the mouths of creeks and gutters. This is harvest time.

Vast beds of flowering water lilies cover the wetlands in masses of yellow, white, red, blue and pink, among iridescent green grasses and sedges. Billabongs and swamps are prime hunting grounds for Aboriginal groups such as the Wagiman, Warray and Woolna. They wade among the lilies, gathering stems, flowers, bulbs and seed pods. As they go, they look for one of the chief freshwater delicacies, long-neck turtle.

Long-necks lay eggs in soft mud at the end of the wet season and continue to feed hungrily until the wetlands begin to dry out at the end of August, when they bury themselves in the mud, to be liberated months later by the first rains.

When water covers the ground people walk in bare feet, feeling for the turtle on the bottom but when the mud is dry, they look for a small airhole or simply poke sticks into the soil. As well as the meat, Aboriginal people enjoy the large deposits of yellow fat the long-neck turtles carry to get through the dry period in their underground chambers.

Traditionally, fire was used to manage the health of country and as a hunting tool. Clan members burned parts of the land on which they travelled, knowing they could return when the plants had regenerated. The burning of thick speargrass attracted insect-feeding wildlife and also made hunting and tracking easier. Today, Aboriginal people move mainly by vehicle but still burn their country for similar reasons.

Pastoralists and conservationists in the north have adopted these traditional land management techniques.

Controlled burning benefits both the landscape and the human inhabitants because most northern plants depend on fire to regenerate. However, late dry season wildfires, usually started by lightning strikes or careless people, are dangerous. Accelerated by introduced grasses that have a higher fuel load than native species, the fires can infiltrate monsoon forests and other delicate habitats, wiping out plants and animals and transforming the landscape into grassland. Aboriginal people knew late dry season fires were ferocious and took great care when burning the land.

The Wardaman, Jawoyn, Alawa and Warlpiri people of the inland are particularly fond of emu and bush turkey, or bustard. Once widespread in the northern woodland, emu are now hard to find because pastoral properties and cattle production have taken over much of the breeding areas.

Most birds gather in wetland areas and are hunted by freshwater people such as the Gunwinggu, Wagiman and Malak Malak (and other clan groups) who enjoy species of ducks and magpie geese, a large black and white bird that was once spread widely throughout Australia but is now limited to the north where a strict hunting season is in force.

In the past, Aboriginal people hunted magpie geese with throwing sticks and small spears but shotguns are used today. The geese can be cooked simply on an open fire but can also be plucked, split through the chest and hung over a raised grill. The breast meat is particularly appreciated.

Main meal in one hand and a salad in the other! Malcolm Wilson of Naiyu community holds aloft a long-neck turtle, while in his other hand are water lily plants that will yield crunchy stems and peanut-like seeds.

## Turtle

*A favourite food of the river people is freshwater turtles which they catch in the local billabong. I was keen to accompany them to their homeland billabong and learn more about some of the aquatic foods such as freshwater mussels, water lily bulbs and stems, file snake and, of course, turtle.*

*We piled into the school truck and off we went 35 kilometres inland to one of the most beautiful billabongs of the Daly River. It was abundant with wildlife and magnificent water lilies. The women were all ready with their hessian bags when I asked, "How are we going to catch turtle ladies?"*

*"Well," the ladies said, "White fella like you need to take all your clothes off and walk in the water up to your waist. Turtle thinks lunch is a nice little worm. White fella be real quick and grab a turtle (mulagu) before turtle grab little worm."*

*Everyone burst out laughing at my expense, but I had my own response, telling them the girls on the island told me the same story when we went to catch mud crabs.*

*We ended up with five fat turtles which were caught with the proper technique by using your feet, sifting through the mud and feeling the turtle. You hope it is not a crocodile!*

## Crocodile

*Another time my two friends asked if I would like to go fishing at the crossing. Not with rods, but spears and a spotlight. I jumped at the chance to spear myself a nice barramundi. That night I picked them up and off we went down the road to the Daly River crossing.*

*The idea was to walk through knee-deep water with the spears while one of the lads shone the spotlight into the water a few metres out from us to spot barramundi.*

*Barramundi are great night feeders. They are known to move up and down the crossing looking for food. When the light hits them, their eyes shine red and then you have to be fast and accurate with the spear.*

*The lads usually get a few barramundi up to 15kg, but this night there was nothing. We decided to walk in a little deeper and give it another go along the crossing when suddenly the spot light picked up a set of red eyes. My mate was ready to throw the spear when the spotlighter said, "Not a barra it's a big croc." The*

spears dropped and we legged it across the water. You should have seen our faces – white as ghosts. The croc was large, around four metres. He missed out on supper that night and so did we.

## Rock Python

*I was sitting down to lunch under a giant mango tree with the ladies from Daly River and we were talking in general about food and some of their favourite tucker.*

*One of the ladies told the group that rock python is a favourite and went about telling us how she uses a wire hook to prod inside crevices in the nearby hills and hook out a python which is quickly dispatched by clubbing it with a stick.*

*I was sitting quietly intrigued by the story when another of the ladies said, "No we don't do that. I am not silly. I take my 22 rifle and poke that in the hole. When the snake comes out I shoot him between the eyes because once one old man went catching python with his wire hook and he prodded out a king brown snake and it bit him. He's lucky to be alive."*

Accompanied by children of the community, chef Steve Sunk and several students from Naiyu head home after a successful hunt.

*This is a favourite dish with the Daly River people. Magpie geese are plentiful in the area and are hunted in season. The gander (male) is the most popular and can be identified by the three to four windpipes. The windpipes and the tail are the favourite parts for roasting on the open fire.*

# Home Style Magpie Goose

### Equipment

bowls
camp oven or heavy based pot
cook's knife
cutting board
measuring cups
measuring spoons
potato masher
vegetable peeler
wooden spoon

### Ingredients

1 magpie goose, cleaned, plucked and gutted
4 medium carrots
4 medium parsnips
2 brown or white onions
4 tablespoons olive or canola oil
4 cups water mixed with 3 chicken stock cubes
2 bay leaves
1 cup sour cream (250ml container)
salt and pepper

### Method

1. Cut goose into eight pieces. Cut legs and breasts into two pieces each.

2. Wash, peel and roughly chop carrots, parsnips and onions.

3. Put oil in camp oven or heavy based pot and heat on medium.

4. Pat goose pieces on a dry paper towel and place in pot. Seal goose to light brown colour.

5. Add vegetables and stir. Pour in water with stock cubes. Add bay leaves and bring to the boil.

6. Skim off any scum, then simmer with lid on until goose is tender. This can take up to 2 hours, especially if goose is an old gander (male) which is very tasty.

7. Remove goose meat when cooked.

8. Mash vegetables and mix in sour cream to form a sauce. Season with salt and pepper.

9. Place goose meat in sauce. Serve with rice or boiled bush yams.

**Serves 4**

*Smoking is a popular way of cooking bush meat. Sometimes the meat can be skewered on green sticks and placed around hot smouldering coals and eaten as it cooks. It suits family social activities on weekends and keeps the children busy. The dressing can also be made using other bush foods like wild plum and bush tomatoes. If using Kakadu or billy goat plum use extra sugar as this fruit is quite tangy.*

# Smoked Crocodile Salad with Rye Berry Vinaigrette

## Equipment
bowl
colander
cook's knife
cutting board
measuring cups
measuring spoons
smoke box
tray or baking dish

## Ingredients
1 large crocodile tail fillet, trimmed and cut in half or 2kg chicken fillet
½ cup salt
1 cup sugar
2 tablespoons wattle seed
1 bag sawdust, used for smoking

## Salad
1 lettuce
2 tomatoes, sliced or wedged
1 small cucumber, thinly sliced
1 lemon, cut into wedges

## Dressing
½ cup white wine vinegar
½ cup olive or canola oil
2 bush limes, juiced
½ cup mixed rye berries or wild berries in season
3 tablespoons sugar
salt and pepper

## Method
1. Pat dry crocodile fillet with paper towel.

2. Mix salt, sugar and wattle seed together and place liberal amounts on both sides of fillet. Place on tray and set aside for 1 hour to cure meat and improve flavour.

3. Fill the sawdust tray and place fillet on smoke box rack. Place the box over a small fire (better done outside). Sawdust will smoulder, cooking and smoking the crocodile fillets until golden brown. Smoking can take up to 25 minutes. Set aside to cool.

4. In a bowl, whisk or beat vinegar, oil and lime juice until mixture thickens.

5. Add berries and sugar. Season with salt and pepper and let stand for 1 hour to enhance berry flavours.

6. Wash and drain lettuce, tear into bite-size pieces.

7. Arrange lettuce, tomatoes and cucumber on a plate. Cut crocodile tail into hand-size fillets, place on top.

8. Pour liberal amounts of dressing over the dish. Garnish with lemon wedges.

## Serves 4

*Barramundi is a very important food for the river and sea people. It is also part of the Dreaming and its image is often found painted on cave walls. This dish can be cooked in a ground oven or next to burning coals if no oven is available. This is a popular cooking method that steams the fish in the paperbark, keeping in the flavours and giving the fish a unique woody flavour.*

# Baked Billabong Barra

## Equipment
cook's knife
cutting board
string
wooden skewer

## Ingredients
2 medium barramundi, cleaned and scaled
salt and pepper
5 spring onions, sliced
2 red capsicums, cut into strips
juice of 3 lemons
large pieces of paperbark

## Method
1. Cut slits into the barramundi and season with salt and pepper. Sprinkle with the spring onions, capsicum and lemon juice.

2. Wrap in damp paperbark. Tie the ends with string and place in hot oven - 200°C. Cook for 25 to 30 minutes depending on fish size. Check with wooden skewer to ensure fish is cooked.

3. Serve with rice.

**Serves 4**

*Wild spinach is used for cooking, medicinal purposes and is also smoked like tobacco. It has a peppery flavour. This is a simple, nutritious dish that can be varied with other white meats such as fish, chicken and prawns. Emu eggs are also good for this recipe.*

# Wild Greens and Crocodile Frittata

## Equipment
bowl
cook's knife
cutting board
camp pan or fry pan with shallow sides
measuring cups
measuring spoons
fork
wooden spoon
wooden skewer

## Ingredients
2 tablespoons olive or canola oil
6-12 bush onions, finely chopped (if not in season 1 small onion)
1 cup crocodile meat, cut into strips
1 cup wild spinach, roughly chopped
5 eggs
3 tablespoons milk, fresh or powder
salt and pepper

## Method

1. Heat medium-sized camp pan with oil, add bush onions and lightly brown.

2. Add crocodile meat and cook until tender. Add wild spinach and toss lightly with wooden spoon. Reduce heat to low.

3. In a bowl, mix eggs with milk, salt and pepper to taste. Whisk with a fork. Pour mixture over crocodile and wild spinach. Mix well.

4. Place pan in hot oven 180-200ºC for 10 minutes or until cooked. Test with wooden stick or skewer. Mixture will rise and be firm.

5. Serve with a salad or roasted yams.

## Serves 2

*Crocodile meat is not eaten by all Aboriginal people as it is a totem for certain clans. Some of the old ladies say that they don't want to eat crocodile as it may have eaten one of their relatives in the past. It is still a traditional food source for many and the freshwater crocodile is most popular (maybe because they don't eat people). The eggs are also enjoyed and are harvested during October and November.*

# Chargrilled Crocodile Tail with Bush Tomato Chutney

### Equipment
bush pan
cook's knife
cutting board
metal skewer

### Ingredients
1 crocodile tail fillet from 5ft crocodile or 2 kg of chicken fillets
salt and pepper
2 tablespoons olive or canola oil

### Method
1. Cut crocodile into small fillets, two hand-sized pieces to a portion. Season meat with salt and pepper.

2. Lightly burn crosses into the crocodile meat with heated skewer or fencing wire.

3. Heat oil in bush pan or on barbecue plate. Fry crocodile for 4-5 minutes both sides, or until cooked (time will depend on thickness of fillets).

4. Serve with bush tomato chutney.

Serves 4

## Bush Tomato Chutney
### Equipment
cook's knife
cutting board
measuring cups
measuring spoons
medium pot
vegetable peeler
wooden spoon

### Ingredients
2 cups dried bush tomatoes
2 tablespoons olive or canola oil
2 red onions, thinly sliced
2 green apples, peeled and small diced
1 cup fresh or frozen mango pulp
1 cup cider vinegar
1 cup brown sugar
1 tablespoon fresh or powdered ginger
1 teaspoon chilli powder
1 cup dry raisins

### Method
1. Chop dry bush tomatoes into small pieces.

2. Heat oil in pot. Add red onions and cook until clear.

3. Add bush tomatoes, apple and mango. Stir with wooden spoon and cook until soft.

4. Add cider vinegar, brown sugar, ginger and chilli. Cook on low heat until a syrup forms. The liquid will thicken like jam. Stir for about 10 minutes. If chutney thickens too quickly, add water.

5. Finally, add the raisins and cook until soft.

### Makes 6 cups

*This dish is fantastic with turtle tripe (stomach) which has been cleaned, cut into small pieces, fried, and placed in the soup. If turtle is not available, oxtail can be used or shin (gravy) beef. If fresh vegetables are not available, use frozen mixed vegetables.*

# Turtle Broth

## Equipment
2 litre plastic bottle
bowls
camp oven
cook's knife
cutting board
measuring spoons
sieve
soup ladle
vegetable peeler

## Ingredients
2 large carrots
2 large onions
2 leeks
2 sticks celery
2 tablespoons olive or canola oil
2 chunks saltwater or freshwater turtle meat with bone (hand sized)
2 chicken cubes
6 litres water, use 3 x 2 litre plastic milk bottles
2 bay leaves
1 tablespoon dry thyme
12 peppercorns
salt and pepper
turtle stomach (tripe)

## Method

**1.** Peel, wash and roughly chop carrots, onion, leek and celery.

**2.** Add oil to camp oven or large pan, heat, then add turtle meat and vegetables. Cook until brown (10-15 minutes).

**3.** Add water and chicken cubes, bring to the boil and skim off any scum. Add bay leaves, thyme and peppercorns. Simmer (slow cook) 2-3 hours or until turtle meat is tender.

**4.** Strain liquid and set aside, use cloth if strainer is not available. Cut meat into bite size pieces. Cut vegetables into small pieces. Place meat back in camp oven with the liquid (stock), heat and season with salt and pepper.

**5.** Cut turtle stomach into small pieces. Heat oil and fry stomach in pan until crisp. Add to turtle soup. Ladle soup into bowls.

**Serves 6**

*This recipe combines the tender breast meat of the magpie goose from the river region with the bush peach which comes from the Pitjantjatjara lands. This glaze can be used for meats like magpie goose, kangaroo, wallaby, goanna and chicken.*

# Pan-Fried Magpie Goose Breast with a Bush Peach Glaze

**Equipment**
cook's knife
cutting board
heavy pan
measuring spoons

**Ingredients**
2 tablespoons olive or canola oil
2 magpie goose breasts, boned and trimmed
salt and pepper

**Method**
1. Heat oil in pan.

2. Place goose breast in pan and brown on low heat, turning until all sides are cooked (about 8 minutes). Season with salt and pepper.

3. Let meat rest for 2 minutes.

4. Place meat on plate and cut breasts into halves or serve whole. Drizzle with ample bush peach glaze.

**Serves 2**

## Bush Peach Glaze
**Equipment**
bowl
grater
juicer
measuring cups
measuring spoons
small pot
wooden spoon

**Ingredients**
3 cups water
1 cup sugar
1 lemon or lime, grated rind, plus juice
1 cup bush peach (quandong), dried or fresh (if dried soak in water until soft)
1 tablespoon cornflour mixed with ¼ cup water to make a paste
2 tablespoons wild honey (sugar bag) or normal honey

**Method**
1. Place water, sugar, lemon or lime juice and rind in pot and bring to the boil.

2. Add bush peach and simmer for 5 minutes until liquid turns red and bush peach becomes soft.

3. Combine cornflour paste and bush peach mixture and stir until it thickens to pouring consistency.

4. Add sugar bag for taste and serve with meat.

*This is a favourite dish with the Daly River people. When the mangoes are in season we slice the mango and add it to the pancakes. The wild purple plums that grow around Woolliana are also good. Sugarbag is wild honey from the stingless bee that lives across the Northern Territory. The ladies check the tree by listening for the humming of the bees. A hole is made in the tree and the honey runs out; it is usually eaten on the spot. The yellow honeycomb is also eaten, but only in small quantities as the ladies say that too much gives a headache. If sugarbag is not available, use honey from the store.*

# Wattle Seed Pancakes with Sugarbag Caramel

**Equipment**
large bowl
measuring cups
measuring spoons
metal spatula or egg flip
small frying pan
soup ladle
whisk or hand beater

**Ingredients**
4 cups self raising flour (blue can)
1 tablespoon baking powder
6 eggs
3 cups milk
3 tablespoons wattle seed
1 quantity Sugarbag Caramel

**Method**
1. Place flour, baking powder, eggs, milk and wattle seed in a bowl. Mix well using handbeater or whisk until there are no lumps. Mixture should be thick like batter; extra milk may be needed.

2. Let rest for 30-60 minutes. Mix again before use.

3. In a hot oiled pan pour a ladle of the mixture and cook both sides until light brown. Place on a plate. Repeat until all batter is cooked.

4. Serve with Sugarbag Caramel.

**Serves 6**

## Sugarbag Caramel
**Equipment**
small pot
measuring cups
wooden spoon

**Ingredients**
2 cups sugar
1 cup water
2 small containers long life cream
1 cup sugarbag (wild honey)

**Method**
1. Boil sugar and water in pot until light brown.

2. Add cream and stir quickly. The mixture will bubble up as it thickens and gets darker.

3. Remove from heat and stir in sugarbag. Cool and thicken.

*The wallaby is a main food for river and coastal people as kangaroo is scarce in these regions. The texture of the meat is similar to young beef (veal) and all parts are eaten. The tail is highly prized. It is a versatile meat that can be used for all cooking processes. Some of the older ladies like to roast the stomach over the hot coals. This recipe is served with a wild plum glaze. If the purple plums are out of season, Kakadu plum (billy goat plum) can be used. Remove the stones from the plums and cut back on the lemon or lime juice as the Kakadu plum is very tart. The Kakadu plum is very high in vitamin C.*

# Wallaby Saddle with Wild Plum Sweet Glaze

### Equipment
cook's knife
cutting board
grater
juicer
large pan
measuring cups
measuring spoons
wooden spoon

### Ingredients
2 tablespoons olive or canola oil
2 whole boned wallaby saddles
salt and pepper

### Sauce
2 tablespoons butter
¼ cup sugar
zest from 2 oranges, cut to match size
zest from 2 lemons or limes, cut to match size
2 cups orange juice
2 lemons or limes, juiced
2 cups wild plum (purple fruit)

### Method

**1.** Heat oil in pan.

**2.** Seal wallaby saddle and cook quickly until medium. Set aside, season lightly with salt and pepper.

**3.** To make the sauce, add butter and sugar to a pan or pot. Cook on low heat until light brown, stirring constantly with wooden spoon.

**4.** Add sliced lemon and orange zest and mix.

**5.** Pour in lemon and orange juice and bring to the boil.

**6.** Add plums and simmer for 5 minutes until sauce thickens and becomes rich red.

**7.** To serve, cut wallaby saddles in chunky pieces, place on a plate and add sauce. Serve with bush yams.

**Serves 4**

*Water lily is used as a vegetable and the stems taste like celery. It is prolific in billabongs where the large crocodiles live. The young shoots that are pale in colour are the best. The bulb is a prize. It is roasted on the fire and tastes similar to potato.*

# Water Lily Salad with Red Claw Yabbies

## Equipment

bowl
cook's knife
cutting board
fork or whisk
heavy pan
measuring cups
measuring spoons

## Ingredients

2 cups water lily stems, pale colour ones
½ cup water lily pod seeds, peeled
8 red claw yabbies, split in half and grilled in a pan or over coals

### Dressing

½ cup balsamic vinegar
¼ cup olive or canola oil
2 tablespoons capers
1 chilli, finely chopped
1 clove garlic, peeled and crushed
salt and pepper

## Method

1. Wash water lily stems thoroughly and cut into finger-sized pieces.

2. Make dressing; whisk the balsamic vinegar and oil together, add capers, chilli and garlic. Mix well and lightly season with salt and pepper.

3. Place water lily stems in bowl with dressing for 10 minutes.

4. To serve, place a serve of the stems on a plate or bowl and drizzle with dressing. Add lily pod seeds then arrange the yabbie halves on top. Decorate with water lily flower.

**Serves 2**

*The old ladies love their traditional way of cooking on the coals but enjoy eating the turtle liver and crispy turtle tripe risotto that was cooked in the classroom. You can make the same dish using chicken livers. You can add some long life cream to the rice before mixing in the turtle liver and tripe.*

# Turtle Liver Risotto with Crispy Turtle Tripe and Pilaf Rice

## Equipment
bowl
camp pan or frying pan
cook's knife
cutting board
measuring spoons
wooden spoon
measuring cups

## Ingredients
1 onion, finely shredded
3 tablespoons olive or canola oil
4 slices lean bacon, rind removed and diced
½ cup sliced mushrooms
1 tablespoon dry mixed herbs
livers from 5 long or short neck turtles, cleaned and cut in half
salt and pepper
tripe from 5 long or short neck turtles, cleaned and crispy fried in olive oil

## Method
1. Fry onion in oil in camp pan until onion is clear, then add bacon and cook until crisp.

2. Add mushrooms and stir in the mixed herbs.

3. Dry livers with a paper towel to stop liquid spitting. Add turtle livers to pan and cook gently. Season with salt and pepper and set aside when cooked.

4. Cut crispy tripe into bite size pieces and mix with liver.

5. Mix ingredients with pilaf rice (page 108) and serve.

**Serves 4**

*Most freshwater mussels are found in the billabongs and are available year round. The ladies dig them up with their feet. Traditionally the mussels are roasted on the fire to open the shells. They have a muddy flavour. To remove the gritty texture and earthy taste, soak the mussels overnight in salt water.*

# Freshwater Mussel Curry

## Equipment
basin
camp oven
cook's knife
cutting board
measuring cups
measuring spoons
wooden spoon

## Ingredients
48 fresh water mussels
2 tablespoons olive or canola oil
2 medium onions
2 cloves garlic
4 tablespoons curry powder from the store
2 hot chillies, seeds removed
2 tablespoons tomato paste
2 cups of good fish stock ( see page 108)
1 tin coconut milk
salt and pepper

## Method

1. Clean mussels by soaking overnight in basin of salty water (1 tablespoon salt: 4 cups water) to remove mud and muddy flavour.

2. Boil the mussels in camp oven and remove meat as shell opens. Set aside. Wash in fresh water when cool.

3. Finely chop onions, garlic and chillies.

4. Heat oil in camp oven and fry onions and garlic until light brown.

5. Stir in curry powder. Add chillies and tomato paste.

6. Pour in fish stock and bring to the boil. Skim off any scum.

7. Simmer for 20 minutes adding extra fish stock as needed.

8. Pour in coconut milk and cook for another 5 minutes or until thick.

9. Add mussel meat and cook for 5 minutes. Season with salt and pepper and serve with pilaf rice (page 108).

**Serves 4**

*This is a marvellous dish we created at the Daly River community where there is an abundant supply of large barramundi and fresh water prawns. Barak and Ronald speared the barramundi at the crossing while Theresa caught the prawns in the billabong. The students wanted to combine their ingredients to create a superb dish, which they did. It is best to make the bisque first. The crisp Water Lily Salad with Red Claw Yabbies goes well with the dish. If prawns are not available, red claw yabbies will do.*

# Barramundi with Freshwater Prawn Bisque

### Equipment
camp pan or frying pan
cook's knife
cutting board
egg flip
flat tray
measuring cups
measuring spoons
wooden skewer

### Ingredients
4 hand-sized pieces barramundi fillets
½ cup plain flour for coating
3 tablespoons olive or canola oil
3 tablespoons butter or margarine
20 freshwater prawns, peeled and deveined (keep the heads and shells for the bisque)
1 quantity of prawn bisque (see page 109)
salt and pepper

### Method
1. Lightly coat barramundi in seasoned flour. Set aside.

2. Place oil and butter in a pan and heat. Flip the barramundi in the pan so both sides are oiled.

3. Cook barramundi until both sides are light brown. Add prawns and cook. Use a wooden skewer to test - when cooked skewer will exit flesh smoothly.

4. Place the barramundi on plate with five prawns. Coat fish with prawn bisque and top with claws to decorate.

5. Serve with water lily salad.

**Serves 4**

*The people from Daly River use barramundi heads and carcass in this recipe.*

# Fish Stock

**Equipment**
colander
cook's knife
cutting board
large pan
measuring cups
measuring spoons
wooden spoon

**Ingredients**
2 tablespoons olive or canola oil
3 medium onions, finely chopped
1 leek, sliced thin
2 large fish heads, remove gills and wash
8 cups (2 litres) cold water
½ teaspoon thyme, dry from store
12 peppercorns
1 bay leaf

**Method**
**1.** Heat oil in pan. Add onions and leek, fry lightly.

**2.** Add fish heads and cold water. Bring to the boil. Skim off any scum.

**3.** Add herbs, peppercorns and bay leaf. Simmer for 20 minutes. Strain ready to use. Do not over-cook as stock becomes bitter.

*Rice is encouraged as a staple food as a lot of the bush starches are seasonal.*

# Pilaf Rice

**Equipment**
cook's knife
cutting board
fork
measuring cups
measuring spoons
sieve
small camp pot with lid
wooden spoon

**Ingredients**
2 cups long grain rice
2 tablespoons olive or canola oil
1 small onion, chopped
salt and pepper
8 cups boiling water
1 chicken cube

**Method**
**1.** Rinse rice in sieve under cold running water to wash out dust and starch. Drain thoroughly.

**2.** In small pot heat oil and gently cook onion until soft and golden.

**3.** Add rice and stir with wooden spoon. Season with salt and pepper. Keep stirring until rice is translucent or shiny.

**4.** Pour boiling water with chicken cube over mixture and bring to boil again. Lower the heat. Cook with lid on for 10-15 minutes or until liquid is absorbed and rice is tender. Fluff with a fork.

*The fresh water prawns, also known as cheripin, are a delicacy. They can grow up to 60cm long and are found in the billabongs.*

# Freshwater Prawn Bisque

## Equipment
camp oven or frying pan
cook's knife
cutting board
large pot
measuring cups
measuring spoons
oven tray
sieve
soup ladle
wooden spoon

## Ingredients
heads, shells and nippers of 20 freshwater prawns
2 tablespoons olive or canola oil
1 large carrot, cut into small cubes
2 sticks celery, cut into thin slices
1 large onion, rough chopped
3 tablespoons tomato paste
1 teaspoon thyme, dry from the store
1 bay leaf
12 peppercorns
4 cups fish stock (see recipe page 108)
salt and pepper

## Method
1. Place the prawn heads, shells and nippers on an oven tray. Roast in oven for 10-15 minutes or until pink and dry.

2. Heat oil in a camp oven or frying pan. Add prawn heads, shells and nippers. Break up with a wooden spoon.

3. Add vegetables, tomato paste, herbs, peppercorns and bay leaf. Fry for three minutes.

4. Pour in fish stock and bring to the boil. Skim off any scum then slow-cook 25 to 30 minutes.

5. Strain liquid into large pot. The liquid should be slightly thick and red in colour. If not, reduce until liquid coats a spoon.

6. Season to taste with salt and pepper and keep warm.

> The Ngura Wiru is our land. This is where we live and hunt. It provides us with wild fruits, berries and tjala (honeyants) depending on the rain. We hunt tinka (goanna), ngintaka (perentie), kalaya (emus), kipara (bush turkey) and our favourite is malu (kangaroo). The best part is the tail. Tjarpa (witchetty grubs) are a favourite food which we collect all year round. The desert shows many colours over the year. In winter the goanna sleeps deep in the red sand burrows, and wakes in the warm spring. The desert comes alive after it rains.

Nora Campbell and Sarah Entata
Tjikala Community

*Desert*

No two seasons in central Australia are ever the same.

During a drought the landscape appears barren and dry, colonised by endless clumps of low, spiky tussocks of spinifex grass and dead or dying mulga trees, black and bent like dilapidated scarecrows.

Yet in a good season, when the earth has soaked up the summer rains, it's a different place. Healthy spinifex can resemble fields of wheat, with flower stems catching the

light, casting a golden sheen over a red landscape. The mulga is thick and green, while a dazzling carpet of wildflowers covers the desert floor.

The vibrancy of blue sky, red earth, yellow, pink and white flowers combines to produce such splendour that central Australia during a good season is one of the most beautiful places on earth.

But as splendid as it can be, the environment is also unforgiving.

In the centuries before European settlement, regular droughts kept a lid on the population of people from tribal groups such as the Arrente, Pitjantjatjara, Luritja, Anmatyerre, Pintupi, Anmatyerre, Alyawarre and Kaytej. However, living within their means was surprisingly easy for small groups during an average or good year; even in tough times the desert was more plentiful than non-indigenous people might think.

Areas around large, permanent waterholes were often sacred, protected by cultural lore much like national parks are protected today by common law; hunting in these places was frowned upon because the areas served as plant and animal reservoirs from which the country could regenerate after a long dry spell. These special places were often held in reserve by Aboriginal people and used as refuges during severe droughts.

After a season of good rain, families could travel into remote, normally waterless areas for short periods to search for food in places they may not have visited for years. In an average year, country with semi-permanent water was rich in resources and the place where desert dwellers spent most of their time.

Traditionally, men hunted larger creatures like kangaroo, goanna, emu and bush turkey while women gathered the main staples – insects, seeds, fruits, yams, small reptiles and marsupials. There was never any guarantee the men would be successful and often survival depended on the women and their expert gathering techniques. As a result, Aboriginal women had a very big say about where and when clan groups travelled.

In desert society, men stayed in their traditional country while women moved from the area of their birth when they married. This ensured that knowledge about plants and gathering was spread widely throughout the Red Centre and clans knew the country and terrain well beyond their horizon.

The accumulation of knowledge over generations means the indigenous people of central Australia possess highly specialised skills in tracking, hunting and gathering and

Clockwise from top left: Police Station waterhole in the Davenport Ranges remains an important site for Kaytej and Alyawarre people who have used it and other desert waterholes for thousands of years. It is one of the few reliable watering points for hundreds of kilometres and is now part of Davenport Ranges National Park; bush tomatoes are a delicacy in desert areas. They flourish after rains and are often picked, dried and stored for eating later; spinifex pigeons live permanently in one area and are noted for their beautiful plumage and tufted topknot. They live off the fallen seeds of grasses, shrubs and trees and are usually found near water; women and children from Kaytej and Alyawarre clans walk through Karlu Karlu (formerly known as Devils Marbles), a popular place for native figs and other desert fruits that grow in the shelter of the large boulders.

have detailed information about animal and plant species and where to find water. While kangaroo was the main animal food for desert people, much of their diet came from more than 140 edible plants.

The purple fruit of the bush tomato is still popular and contains high levels of vitamin C. The tomato is found on a shrub that grows one metre high and bears grey-green leaves and purple flowers. With some species, the fruit has to be split open to remove a mass of black seeds. The bush tomato can be dried and stored for long periods and is prolific in a good season.

Women and children spread far and wide to collect two common varieties (one round, the other oval) and, in remote communities today, dried bush tomatoes are a popular alternative to chips and chocolate.

Aboriginal people still gather large amounts of the desert raisin, which comes from the same (Solanum) family as the bush tomato. Traditionally, bush raisins were ground into a thick paste, rolled into a ball and left to dry in the sun. Balls were often stored along trails or near camping areas for future use.

Wild fig is still popular and native gooseberry was once widespread; the ripe native plum looks like a small black olive. The popular bush banana grows on a woody, snaking vine. The fruit is long and flat like a slim mango and is sweet when green and immature. The mature fruit can be roasted and eaten. The bush banana's leaves and roots are also eaten while the fine, feathery seed plumes are used for ceremonial decoration.

One of the most sought-after, and sweetest, fruits is the quandong or native peach, which has twice as much vitamin C as an orange. The fruit is fleshy and bright red; tart when immature but very sweet when ripe. Unfortunately, the quandong tree is not fire tolerant and feral animals such as camels and donkeys have over-grazed many desert areas where the quandong was once found.

In an environment that swings between drought and plenty, many desert plants produce large amounts of seed to ensure survival. In the past, the seeds were an important source of protein, oils, vitamins and fibre for desert people who collected from about 70 plant species, including grasses.

Wattles, or acacias, make up many of the desert shrubs and, of that family, mulga is one of the most common trees in central Australia. Mulga wood is strong and easily worked when green and is used by desert people for boomerangs, fighting clubs, shields, digging sticks and churingas (sacred boards).

Before the arrival of Europeans, mulga seeds were an important part of the Aboriginal diet – they were gathered and ground into flour, mixed with water to create a paste that tastes like peanuts, shaped into small loaves and cooked in coals to produce damper or unleavened bread. Grass seeds were also collected and ground, although they needed a lot of work to separate the seed from plant debris.

Some desert women still gather seeds to bake into bread rather than use flour. While seeds and fruit are readily available during the good times, other foods such as tubers (yams) and bulbs can be found underground even during drought. Many of these plants are buried deeply and require considerable effort to reach, but they hold significant amounts of water and were often responsible for the survival of families during the worst of times (along with water-retaining frogs that burrow into the earth, trees that hold water in hollows created by insect borers, and remote wells).

The Pintupi people were particularly adept desert survivors, ranging across a large dry area of the western desert. They knew of remote wells and how to find plants and animals that contained life-sustaining moisture.

A long yellow yam, known in some parts of central Australia as the bush carrot, is widely collected while the bush potato, a large, fleshy tuber, is eaten raw or cooked in the coals of a fire. Bush onions are small, sweet bulbs usually found on the sides of creek beds that can be eaten raw or cooked lightly.

Hunters must be skilled to locate these plants. A sign of their presence could be as insignificant as a small crack in the earth, the remnant of an aerial shoot or a different sound to the ground when hit with a digging stick.

The witchetty bush, another acacia, is home to one of the great delicacies of the desert, the witchetty grub, a moth larva that bores into long, shallow roots and is the largest insect eaten by Aboriginal people.

Desert people can detect the presence of witchetty grubs by cracks in the earth around the bush and swelling of the roots. These days, women use steel rods with flattened ends to dig through the earth and crack open the roots; traditionally, they used mulga digging sticks.

The creamy-white grubs are thrown on hot coals, rolled lightly for a minute or two and eaten. High in protein and fat, they vary in taste from region to region — some grubs taste like cheese while others have a nutty flavour. The witchetty grub is an important food for desert people, particularly for young, growing children. Roots containing the grubs are sometimes broken off, unopened, and stored for several days or weeks.

Page 117, L to R: Marlene Jones Nambin, Rosie Thomson Nakamarra, Winnie Martin Nangala, Norma Joshua Nangala and Joy Waistcoat Nambin examine a native fig tree at Karlu Karlu, south of Tennant Creek.

Previous page: Witchetty grubs are an important source of food in the desert. They are found in the roots of the witchetty bush; Aboriginal women dig the roots with a long metal rod, crack open the root and either cook the insect on the spot in coals, or take them home. The highly nutritious insect is important bush tucker for growing children.

These pages, clockwise from top left: Wild flowers erupt into bloom in central Australia; in sheaths of plastic, kangaroo tails lie ready to be put on a fire at Titjikala for a community celebration. Kangaroo tails are equivalent to currency in many desert communities in central Australia and some aspiring politicians have been known to distribute them to communities before elections; silver service in the desert: an upmarket tourist camp at Titjikala features dining on the red sands and local bush tucker; A kangaroo is cooked the traditional way — lightly roasted in the coals; Aboriginal men return from a walk in the Tanami Desert with sand goannas that will go on the fire for a morning 'smoko' along with a mug of strong black tea.

Sweet foods are rare in the desert but they can be found, particularly in the good times when plants are flowering. Native bees build hives in the hollows of tree trunks and honey ants store nectar in their abdomens. Flowers from the grevillea are sucked or soaked in water to produce a sweet drink.

Fire is used for warmth and cooking and to manage the land. Burnt areas generate green shoots that attract animals while scorched country is easy to track across.

Landscapes that are burned regularly in a mosaic or scattered fashion can be protected from major wildfires because fuel loads are low.

Arrente, Luritja and Pitjantjatjara people tracked, hunted and ate animals such as kangaroos, perenti (giant goanna), goannas, porcupines (echidna), snakes, lizards and birds such as emus, bush turkeys, spinifex pigeons, budgerigars and crows. Most animals were cooked ceremonially on a fire or in the coals, with everyone in the community receiving a portion. Today, kangaroos are still cooked in their skins to retain moisture and juices.

Traditionally, desert people ate every part of an animal. Until recently, even the bones were ground down and eaten. Larger bones and sinews were used to make weapons and hunting implements.

Kangaroo tails, which are frozen and sold in community stores today, are a favourite part of the animal because they contain large amounts of tasty fat. Traditionally, kangaroos and emus were speared but today they are shot. Goannas are still dug or smoked out of their shallow holes.

The imposing northern wall of the MacDonnell Ranges that runs east and west of Alice Springs. Desert people often sheltered among the ranges during harsh times. Clumps of spinifex grass grow abundantly among the rocky and sandy terrain. The grasses provide shelter for many small animals and food for countless insects, birds and reptiles. Before the arrival of Europeans in the centre, Aboriginal women painstakingly harvested and separated the seed, ground it into flour, and made a form of damper.

Rabbits preceded the arrival of Europeans to the Red Centre and became a popular dish with desert people until recent eradication by the calici virus. Another animal that is part of desert life is the 'pussycat', or feral cat. It is likely cats arrived via Western Australia from shipwrecked Dutch vessels or may have been brought to the north by Macassan trepangers, centuries before British settlement.

The influence of indigenous women in desert commnities waned after European settlement in the 1800s. Traditional lifestyles changed further with the advent of motor vehicles and firearms and today there are few desert people who live entirely off bush tucker, but many still gather and hunt traditional food.

There is a huge demand for bush tucker from restaurants and food companies. Acacia seed is being gathered again; not to be ground into flour for damper but for ice-cream flavouring; demand for bush tomato and quandong far outstrips supply. Aboriginal people collect for these markets because it generates income for their communities and suits their outdoor lives and traditional values.

While much desert bush tucker finds its way interstate and overseas, much is still eaten on Aboriginal communities where it is highly valued.

This page: Charles Darwin University chefs Steve Sunk and Lee Harding find themselves in some remote locations when taking courses to Northern Territory Aboriginal communities. Travelling by 4WD and utility truck and cooking in the sand dunes are common.

Opposite page: A desert storm looms over Karlu Karlu NP, also known as Devils Marbles.

## Wild Cat

*While teaching in the Tanami Desert region I had the opportunity to go hunting with the older ladies. They are great and have a wealth of knowledge about the desert. They are fantastic hunters and gatherers.*

*This day we were looking for wild cat, so into the Troopie (Toyota Troopcarrier, a commonly used outback vehicle) with plenty of water we drove out to the nearby homelands (a special place for Aboriginal people of that area). We came across a large cat. The women said, "Run it down!" Which meant follow him until he tires out. So I did.*

*As the cat began to slow up the women said, "Stop". They all piled out with their sticks which are used as clubs. They chased the cat into a circle and closed in on it – close enough to club it. One whack and it was all over. The ladies cheered.*

*They then picked up dry timber and made a fire and threw the cat into it to burn off the hair. They then slow-roasted the cat on the coals while the billy tea was boiling. So lunch consisted of roasted cat and billy tea.*

*They told me that these cats have been there for 500 years and their ancestors used to hunt them. They probably came off early explorer ships from the west coast and slowly migrated to the desert. The cats are used as a strong medicine for stomach problems. Some say it can help rid the body of cancer and ulcers.*

*I was not going to argue. I enjoyed being out with these ladies with their football club beanies on as they told stories in half their language and English so I could understand. I was starting to learn Walpiri at the time.*

## Goanna Hunt

*On another occasion, the ladies and I went on a goanna hunt. This is a favourite food of Aboriginal people all over Australia, especially these ladies. They love the goanna and also the hunt.*

*With long sticks and wooden clubs we set off into the sand hills which was made up of sparse trees and Spinifex grass. We were looking for dug-out holes where the goannas would sleep during the hot days.*

*When we spotted a deep hole in the sand one of the ladies would poke the sharp stick into the hole. Hopefully a goanna was home to be enticed out and then other ladies would club it over the head. It usually was a hit-and-miss operation and a whole day's hunting may yield one or two nice fat goannas. It is hard work.*

*That day we downed two goannas and a bonus dilly bag of bush bananas. They are similar to a large bean and have the same texture. These grow like vines off the trees and spring out of the ground with the last rain at the end of the wet season. You have to have a keen eye to find them like everything else when you are in the desert.*

*Back to the goannas … it was lunch time. So out comes the billy, a flour tin. All the flour in remote communities comes in tins. The tins come in handy for gathering food and making tea. One of the ladies put the fire on and waited till the wood burned down to hot coals. The goannas were placed on top. The bush bananas were eaten raw as the goannas were slow roasted and occasionally turned.*

*The ladies used a stick to remove the goannas and placed them on some melaleuca branches. They broke the lizards apart and we all ate heartily with plenty of billy tea. Once again a great time and experience was had by all.*

Central desert women (left to right) Trixie Carr Nangala, Winnie Martin Nangala, Barbara Foster Nangala and Norma Joshua Nangala sit on their swags (bed rolls) as they prepare a fire to cook lunch; Steve Sunk scrapes coals from a large damper cooked in the earth; If he can be forced down, a large lizard that has climbed a shrub will be good eating.

*A classic dish using wild kangaroo or wallaby. This recipe also works well with beef. Kangaroo is the favoured meat in the desert. High in fat content, the tail is the most sought after part and is generally roasted on the fire.*

# Kangaroo Bourguignon

### Equipment
bowls
camp oven or large pot
cook's knife
cutting board
frying pan
measuring cups
measuring spoons
wooden spoon

### Ingredients
4 tablespoons olive or canola oil
½ cup small bacon pieces
6 cups diced kangaroo meat (use tender part from the back)
2 cloves garlic or 2 teaspoons of garlic from the jar
2 tablespoons tomato paste
2 tablespoons plain flour
3 cups water with three stock cubes for flavour
1 tablespoon olive or canola oil, extra
24 small peeled onions (same size as pickled onions) or bush onions
2 cups small mushrooms
salt and pepper

### Method
1. Put oil in camp oven and heat.

2. Add bacon and brown. Add diced kangaroo meat and garlic. Seal meat by browning. Stir with wooden spoon.

3. Mix tomato paste and flour then stir into pan until mixed. Add water and stock cubes.

4. Stir until simmering then slow-cook for one hour. Add more water if mixture dries out.

5. Heat the extra tablespoon of oil in frying pan. Add onions and mushrooms and brown lightly. Add to the kangaroo and slow-cook for 30 minutes or until kangaroo is tender.

6. Add salt and pepper to taste. Serve with rice or pasta.

**Serves 8**

*Eastern grey and red kangaroo are mostly eaten in the desert regions. They are hunted on a regular basis. Kangaroo tail is also readily available in community stores. Kangaroo tail is very tasty and similar to oxtail but with good omega type fat. Kangaroo tail can be substituted with kangaroo mince.*

# Kangaroo Tail with Pasta

### Equipment
bowls
cook's knife
cutting board
large camp oven or pan
measuring cups
measuring spoons
wooden spoon

### Ingredients
1 kangaroo tail cut into chunky pieces
4 tablespoons olive or canola oil
3 large onions, finely chopped
2 cloves garlic, crushed
4 fresh tomatoes, chopped (if not available use tinned tomatoes)
2 tins of peeled tomatoes, chopped
3 tablespoons tomato paste
2 tablespoons dry oregano or mixed herbs
1 bay leaf
3 cups water
salt and pepper

### Method
1. Wash kangaroo tail pieces and dry with paper towel.

2. Heat camp oven or pan with oil until hot. Use open fire or stove.

3. Add kangaroo tail pieces and stir until light brown.

4. Remove kangaroo pieces and set aside.

5. In the same pan add onions and garlic and brown lightly. Place kangaroo tail pieces in pan.

6. Stir in fresh and tinned tomato pieces, tomato paste, herbs, bay leaf and water.

7. Bring to the boil. Skim off any scum then simmer (slow-cook) for at least two hours. Replace lost liquid with water as it reduces.

8. Season with salt and pepper. Serve on top of pasta — fettuccine or spaghetti is best.

**Serves 4**

*Bush meats are low in fat and strong in flavour. To make the meat tender, long cooking time is needed. The bush meat pie is a good family meal.*

# Bush Meat Pie with Kangaroo, Bush Turkey and Emu

## Equipment
cook's knife
cutting board
deep baking tray (medium size)
heavy camp oven
ladle
measuring cups
measuring spoons
wooden spoon

## Ingredients
3 cups or 750g kangaroo
3 cups or 750g emu breast
3 cups or 750g bush turkey leg meat
½ cup plain flour (red tin)
3 tablespoons olive or canola oil
1 cup chopped bacon
2 large onions, medium diced
3 cloves garlic, roughly chopped
2 tablespoons tomato paste
2 tablespoons dry mixed herbs
½ cup whole dried bush tomatoes
2 bay leaves
4 cups water
2 beef stock cubes
3 cups sliced mushroom (if fresh not available use tinned mushrooms in butter sauce)
salt and pepper
1 packet short pastry
1 packet puff pastry
1 cup milk

## Method
1. Dice bush meats then coat lightly in flour.

2. Heat oil in heavy camp oven until very hot. Place meat and bacon in oven and brown, stirring constantly. Remove meat and set aside.

3. Brown onions and garlic in camp oven.

4. Add tomato paste, herbs, bush tomatoes and bush meat. Mix with wooden spoon.

5. Add bay leaves and water to just cover the meat. Add beef cubes.

6. Bring to the boil, skim off any scum then slow-cook with lid on. Liquid will thicken slowly. Add water if too thick (sauce should be reddish brown). Cook for 1½ hours or until meat is tender.

7. Add mushrooms and season with salt and pepper. Sauce should be thick. Let filling cool down.

8. Place short crust sheet in baking tray or pie tin for single pies. Add filling, top with puff pastry and brush with milk.

9. Place in a 220ºC oven and cook until golden brown (35-45 minutes).

**Serves 6**

*The bush turkey is a popular meat with the desert people. It is a large bird and has a strong flavour. Long cooking is best for this meat. The Lajamanu ladies asked for other recipes for bush turkey, instead of the favourite roasting on a hot fire. Other dark meat can be used for this dish like stewing steak or lamb. If no conventional oven is available, this dish can be cooked in a camp oven on the coals.*

# Bush Turkey Casserole

## Equipment
bowls
camp oven
casserole or braising dish
cook's knife
cutting board
measuring cups
measuring spoons
vegetable peeler

## Ingredients
3 tablespoons olive or canola oil
2 legs bush turkey, boned and large diced
salt and pepper
2 cups carrots, peeled and large diced
2 cups onion, diced
1 cup celery, diced
3 tablespoons plain flour
1 small tin tomato puree
6 cups water with 2 beef cubes
1 clove garlic, crushed
12 peppercorns
2 bay leaves
12 dried bush tomatoes
6 potatoes, large diced

## Method

1. Heat oil in camp oven. Season meat with salt and pepper and fry brown on all sides. Remove and place in casserole or braising dish.

2. Fry vegetables in camp oven. Add flour and mix well.

3. Add tomato puree, water and stock cubes, garlic, peppercorns, bay leaves and bush tomatoes.

4. Bring to the boil. Skim off any scum and place liquid over meat. Cover with lid or aluminium foil and cook in a moderate oven at 180°C for about two hours or until meat is tender. Liquid can reduce during cooking process; add more water or casserole will be too thick.

5. Add diced potatoes about one hour into cooking. Cook until potatoes are soft and liquid forms a good sauce. Season with salt and pepper.

**Serves 6**

*This is a top family dish that adds extra nutrition to a favourite hunted bird. The feathers of the bush turkey are used for ceremonial dancing.*

# Stuffed Bush Turkey Leg Roasted

## Equipment
bowl
cook's knife
cutting board
measuring cups
measuring spoons
whisk
fry pan
roasting pan or camp oven

## Ingredients
2 bush turkey legs, boned out
8 lean slices bacon (use ham if bacon unavailable)
salt and pepper

### Stuffing
1 tablespoon olive or canola oil
1 onion, chopped finely
1 cup carrot, diced into cubes
1 cup bush peanuts, cleaned and roasted lightly to remove skins, chop rough
2 eggs
1 cup milk
2 cups breadcrumbs
2 tablespoons dry mixed herbs

## Method
1. Lay bush turkey leg meat out and pat flat with a stick or hand. Layer with bacon.

2. To make stuffing, lightly fry onion, carrot and bush peanuts in oil. Cool.

3. Whisk eggs and milk in large bowl or dish. Add breadcrumbs and dry herbs. Mix with onion, carrot and bush peanuts to make a thick moist paste (similar to damper dough).

4. Lay half the stuffing on each leg and form into a roll, folding meat over. Season well with salt and pepper.

5. Tie meat with string to keep shape; alternatively, wrap in aluminium foil and twist the ends. Seal meat in roasting pan and then cook in a hot oven, 200°C for one hour. A camp oven can also be used.

6. Set cooked leg aside for five minutes to allow juices to rest. Slice and serve with mashed potatoes and freshly cooked vegetables. If not available use frozen vegetables.

7. Serve with pan juices.

**Serves 4-6**

*For the desert Titjikala community, witchetty grubs are a staple food source. The old ladies collect the grubs using a metal rod to dig out tree roots where the witchetty grubs live. The grubs are very high in protein and are generally roasted directly on the camp fire.*

# Kangaroo Tail Soup with Witchetty Grubs

## Equipment

2 litre bottle
bowls
camp oven or large pot
colander
cook's knife
cutting board
measuring spoons
meat cleaver
vegetable peeler

## Ingredients

1 kangaroo tail cut into small pieces using meat cleaver
2 tablespoons olive or canola oil
3 whole carrots, washed and peeled
3 onions, roughly chopped
4 sticks celery, cut in half
1 leek, shredded
6 litres water, use 3 x 2 litre plastic milk bottles
2 bay leaves
10 peppercorns
2 beef cubes
18 large witchetty grubs, lightly fried
salt and pepper

## Method

**1.** Wash kangaroo tail pieces, place in the camp oven and top with cold water. Bring to the boil to blanch. Discard water and wash tails again to remove bone and blood.

**2.** Heat camp oven with oil then lightly brown kangaroo tail.

**3.** Add vegetables and water and bring to the boil. Skim off any scum. Add bay leaves, peppercorns and beef cubes.

**4.** Simmer for 3 hours or until the kangaroo tail is tender. As liquid reduces replace with more water.

**5.** Remove large vegetables and slice into smaller pieces, return to camp oven and season with salt and pepper. Cooked frozen vegetables can also be added.

**6.** Serve in bowl and top with three witchetty grubs.

**Serves 6**

*Generally the men cook kangaroo whole in a fire pit and drink the warm blood. When the kangaroo is cooked it is broken into pieces and given to family members. Some groups do this as a special ceremony as the kangaroo is a symbol of the desert people. The haunch part of the kangaroo comprises the upper leg meat and the loin, which is boned in a similar way to the wallaby the river people use. Kangaroo can be purchased at the supermarket or store in some communities. The desert people will only buy the tail, not the other parts.*

# Grilled Kangaroo Steak with Fried Bush Yam, Tomato and Mushroom

### Equipment
bowl or plate
camp pan or fry pan
cook's knife
cutting board
measuring cups
measuring spoons
tongs
wooden spoon

### Ingredients
3 tablespoons olive or canola oil
4 hand size steaks from kangaroo haunch (back part)
1 onion, finely chopped
1 clove garlic, crushed
2 cups mushrooms, sliced
4 tomatoes, blanched and skinned (or 1 tin peeled tomatoes)
1 cup water with 1 beef cube
salt and pepper

### Method
**1.** Heat oil in camp pan or frying pan. Add kangaroo steaks and cook until medium or still bloody inside. Put meat aside and keep warm.

**2.** In the same pan fry onions and garlic until clear, stirring constantly with wooden spoon.

**3.** Add mushrooms and stir until lightly cooked (2-3 minutes) then add tomatoes and liquid stock. Simmer lightly for five minutes.

**5.** Season with salt and pepper. Pour sauce over kangaroo steaks.

**6.** Serve with wedges of bush yams, crisp fried or baked in hot coals. Sweet potato can also be used.

**Serves 4**

*This dish is a favourite of the Lajamanu ladies who often go hunting perentie or sand goanna. They use long sticks which they poke down the holes to drive the goannas out. This is a hearty dish that can be served with roasted bush bananas. Desert python can also be used as it is the same texture as goanna. Chicken is another alternative.*

# Goanna and Vegetable Stew

### Equipment
bowls
camp oven or heavy fry pan
can opener
cook's knife
cutting board
measuring spoons
tongs
wooden spoon

### Ingredients
1 goanna, skinned and chopped in finger length cutlets, washed
salt and pepper
4 tablespoons olive or canola oil
2 cloves garlic, crushed
3 onions, diced in large pieces
3 red capsicums, seeds removed, diced in large pieces
1 tin tomato puree or chopped tomatoes
2 eggplants, diced in large pieces (soak in salty water for 20 minutes to remove bitterness)
3 zucchini, thick sliced
12 small mushrooms, cut in half
1 tablespoon tomato paste

### Method
**1.** Season goanna cutlets with salt and pepper and fry quickly in pan with olive oil until cooked (5-8 minutes). Set aside.

**2.** In camp oven or heavy-based pan, cook onions and garlic for a few minutes without colouring the onions and garlic.

**3.** Add chopped capsicum, cook for several minutes then add the tomato puree or chopped tomatoes.

**4.** Bring to the boil and simmer. Skim off any scum. Drain eggplant and add to the pot. Cook until tender. Add zucchini, mushrooms and tomato paste. Cook until soft.

**5.** Season lightly and serve on a bed of rice.

**Serves 6-8**

*The heads of the witchetty grubs can be removed after you fry them. The older ladies generally eat the lot. The grubs have a nutty-woody flavour and are a great source of protein. Chicken can be substituted for the witchetty grubs.*

# Witchetty Grubs with Pasta

## Equipment
bowls
cook's knife
cutting board
deep frying pan or pot
measuring spoons
wooden spoon

## Ingredients
2 tablespoons olive or canola oil
3 cloves garlic, crushed
24 witchetty grubs
12 medium mushrooms, thinly sliced
2 large tomatoes, roughly chopped
4 spring onions, cut into match length pieces
1 bunch spinach, leaves cut into strips
8 dried, ground bush tomatoes
4 handfuls cooked pasta (fettucine, macaroni – any shape will do)
salt and pepper

## Method
1. Heat oil in a pan or pot. Add garlic and cook lightly.

2. Add witchetty grubs and cook for 3-4 minutes, tossing in pan. The grubs will expand in size.

3. Mix in mushrooms, tomatoes, spring onions and spinach. Cook for 2 minutes or until vegetables are cooked slightly.

4. Add hot pasta and ground dried bush tomatoes. Toss lightly until pasta mixes evenly with the grubs.

5. Season with salt and pepper.

**Serves 4**

*Bush turkey can also be served with wild spinach, braised water lily bulbs or mixed vegetables. The bush tomato grows in the Tanami Desert region and is available between March and May.*

# Bush Turkey Breast Roasted with Bush Tomato Chutney

**Equipment**
bowls
cook's knife
cutting board
deep roasting dish or pot
frying pan
measuring cups
small pot
wooden spoon

**Ingredients**
1 bush turkey breast, boned
1 cup olive or canola oil
salt and pepper
1 cup ground bush tomatoes
1 cup water
2 cups bush tomato chutney
with 1 cup water

**Method**
1. Lightly oil the turkey breast. Season with salt and pepper and coat with ground bush tomatoes.

2. Heat oil in frying pan. Place turkey in pan to seal all parts of breast then remove.

3. Place turkey in baking dish or camp oven and add 1 cup water. Roast at 180°C for 1 hour.

4. Remove meat and cover with cloth or aluminium foil for 5 minutes.

5. While meat is resting, heat bush tomato chutney with 1 cup water.

6. Slice the bush turkey breast and pour chutney over the meat.

**Serves 6-8**

## Bush Tomato Chutney
**Equipment**
cook's knife
cutting board
measuring cups
measuring spoons
medium pot
vegetable peeler
wooden spoon

**Ingredients**
2 cups dried bush tomatoes
2 tablespoons olive or canola oil
2 red onions, thinly sliced
2 green apples, peeled and small diced
1 cup fresh or frozen mango pulp
1 cup cider vinegar
1 cup brown sugar
1 tablespoon fresh or powdered ginger
1 teaspoon chilli powder
1 cup raisins

**Method**
1. Chop dry bush tomatoes into small pieces.

2. Heat oil in pot, add red onions and cook until clear.

3. Add bush tomatoes, apple and mango. Stir with wooden spoon until soft.

4. Add cider vinegar, brown sugar, ginger and chilli. Cook on low heat until a syrup forms. The liquid will thicken like jam. Stir for about 10 minutes. If chutney thickens too quickly, add water.

5. Add raisins and cook until soft.

**Makes 6 cups**

# Bush Baking

Aboriginal women are among the most enthusiastic bakers in Australia.

In the Northern Territory alone, one thousand 10-kilogram tins of flour are sold to the communities each week - red cans for plain flour and blue cans for self-raising flour.

The cans are fitted with tight lids that shut out weevils and moisture that can spoil the flour by causing mould. An empty flour tin is a very useful item in the bush, ideal for mixing food, gathering bush tucker and making billy tea.

Give the ladies some baking powder, flour, powdered milk and water and you have a recipe for damper, a type of bush bread introduced by early white settlers and passed on to Aboriginal women, who already made their own breads from ground plant seeds.

The ladies still bake damper and Johnny cakes in hot coals covered in sand. After thousands of years' experience, they know exactly how long it takes to cook them perfectly.

Damper is removed from the coals and the sand brushed off; it is then broken into pieces, spread with butter and golden syrup and served with black billy tea - a great treat when you are out in the bush.

When I first went to remote communities, it was no surprise to me that Aboriginal ladies did a fantastic job on the scratch mix and yeast-based products such as bread rolls and pizzas; they have excellent kneading skills to break gluten down in the dough which gives a wonderful finish to the food.

The ladies love to incorporate bush fruit seeds - such as wattle seed, pepper berry, bush tomatoes, Kakadu plum and bush yams - to give a very distinctive flavour to the bread.

Rendered fat from dugong, turtle, goanna and bush turkey can also be used to enhance the flavour and give the bread that little extra. Of course, these are protected animals used only by Aboriginal people but other animal fats can be used - try duck or geese, they are very tasty.

Aboriginal people love bread and baking, so hopefully – one day - there will be a bakery in every Aboriginal community employing local people.

It sometimes takes me up to 14 hours to drive to work, along pot-holed roads and dirt. One of my stops is Kalkaringi in the Victoria River district of the Northern Territory. This is where the famous Gurindji walk-off happened, when local Aboriginal people walked off the Vestey-owned cattle stations in protest over low wages and land rights.

I met a great character running the local bakery whose name was Phillip Gigante. Originally a shoemaker by trade, Phil became a brickie and then a baker. Phil is a Melburnian who decided he needed a change, so he visited his brother who was already working in this remote community. He saw an empty bakery and inquired about a job.

Phil trained himself to bake for the community and was soon supplying bread to the people of Daguragu and Kalkaringi. From these humble beginnings started a training program for local indigenous people to bake bread.

A classic situation in the bakery at Daguragu is that when the smell of baking bread wafts outside, wild donkeys come demanding bread by kicking at the door until they get some scraps. Sometimes Phil's dog Jackson chases them away.

As a result of this program, and Phil's ingenuity, local people have fresh bread and the occasional birthday cake. A favourite is Gurindji damper made with bush turkey fat that gives the bread a lovely gamey flavour.

This page: Baking at Daguragu with Phil Gigante.

Previous page: Loaves baked by the women of Wadeye.

*The bush tomato scones come from Laramba community in the Tanami Desert where the bush tomato grows. It is high in vitamin C and has a nice savoury flavour. There are a few different species of bush tomato. One of them the ladies call "cheeky" because they give you a bad stomach ache when you eat them.*

# Bush Tomato Scones

## Equipment
baking tray
bowl
measuring cups
measuring spoons
scone cutter or cup
sieve

## Ingredients
4 cups self raising flour (blue tin)
1 tablespoon baking powder
½ teaspoon salt
2 tablespoons margarine
1 cup chopped dry bush tomatoes
2 cups milk

## Method
1. Sift flour, baking powder and salt into a bowl.

2. Rub in margarine and mix in bush tomatoes.

3. Mix gently to a soft damper dough by adding milk. If a little dry, add extra milk.

4. Pat out dough to the thickness of two fingers, then cut scones with scone cutter or cup.

5. Place scones on lightly oiled baking tray. Brush with milk.

6. Bake in oven at 190ºC for 20 minutes or until golden brown.

7. Serve hot with golden syrup or butter, and billy tea.

**Makes 16 scones**

*This is a simple dish which is popular with the whole family. You can use bush fruits that have been gathered during the day or you can use dried or canned fruits. A favourite with the ladies is quandong or wild peach. Instead of cream over it they also love golden syrup.*

# Bush Pudding

## Equipment
brush
colander
cook's knife
cutting board
4 round ceramic moulds or
aluminium containers
small pot
wooden spoon

## Ingredients
14 slices white or brown bread
6 cups bush berries (wild peach, rosellas) if not available use frozen berries, apples
½ cup sugar
½ cup melted margarine

## Method

**1.** Cut crusts off bread. Cut four round tops and four round bases out of the bread. Cut the remainder of bread into fingers.

**2.** Wash and clean the berries using colander.

**3.** Heat berries and sugar gently in a small pot until liquid runs from berries.

**4.** Brush bread fingers with margarine, line moulds with bread fingers margarine-side against mould.

**5.** Add the round bread base then pour fruit equally into the four bread moulds. Cover with bread top and more margarine.

**6.** Cook in a moderate oven at 180ºC for 25 minutes or until tops are brown. Remove from oven when cooked and let rest for 10 minutes then turn out onto plate.

**7.** Serve with Sugarbag Caramel (see recipe page 97) and cream.

**Serves 4**

*This is an easy way to make bread or bread rolls out in the bush. The bread can be baked in a camp oven as well as in a conventional oven. Bush herbs and fruits such as wattle seed, bush tomato or Kakadu plum can be added to the mix.*

# Basic Bread Scratch Mix

**Equipment**
baking tray
large bowl
brush
cook's knife
cutting board
measuring cup
measuring spoons

**Ingredients**
4 cups plain flour (red tin)
1 tablespoon powdered milk
1 tablespoon dry yeast
2 tablespoons margarine
3 cups warm water
(approximately)

**Method**

**1.** Place dry ingredients in bowl and mix with hands. Add margarine and rub in until flour becomes crumbly.

**2.** Make a well in the middle of the flour. Add water while mixing to a soft dough.

**3.** Place dough on a flour-dusted board or table and knead for 15 minutes or until the dough is fine textured.

**4.** Shape dough into a ball. Cover with damp cloth until dough has doubled in size. This can take up to one hour, depending on room temperature.

**5.** Knock the dough back and knead lightly to remove air.

**6.** Cut dough into two pieces and turn into desired shape.

**7.** Place on lightly oiled baking tray. Brush dough with water, wait until dough has doubled in size.

**8.** Place bread in a preheated 220ºC oven and bake 25-30 minutes or until golden brown.

**Makes 2 loaves**

*A family favourite in the desert, bush fruits are high in vitamins and minerals in comparison with store-bought fruits. This is a basic mix recipe where lots of other fruits and nuts can also be used. The bush coconut tastes like citrus in flavour. It grows on one of the bloodwood trees that are widespread throughout the Tanami Desert. It is an important food as it contains water and a grub sack within the fruit. It looks like a miniature coconut. The pulp can also be used in salad dressings. It is a refreshing treat, especially for children, when served with bush banana.*

# Bush Muffins

## Equipment
bowl
cutting board
measuring cups
measuring spoons
muffin tray
vegetable knife
wooden spoon

## Ingredients
½ cup sugar
2 eggs
¾ cup milk
2 cups self raising flour (blue tin)
1 tablespoon baking powder
1 cup sultanas
6 bush coconuts, scrape insides, keep pulp
½ cup melted margarine or butter (if not available use canola oil)

## Method
**1.** Mix sugar and eggs in a bowl. Beat lightly using wooden spoon then add milk.

**2.** Mix flour and baking powder, sultanas and bush coconut. Add to milk and egg mixture and beat slowly —do not over beat.

**3.** Slowly add melted margarine and stir until mixture looks like smooth thick batter.

**4.** Pour into well-oiled muffin tray and cook 20-25 minutes at 180ºC in preheated oven.

**Makes 12**

# Captions

pages 18-21

A magpie goose examines her eggs at the end of the wet season. If the rains are too strong or a cyclone strikes the Top End, many goose nests are flooded and the eggs destroyed.

Jawoyn boys, their bodies and faces smeared with white clay, dance in a ceremony at Nitmiluk, near Katherine.

A lightning bolt strikes Top End woodland during a tropical storm in the build-up to the monsoon. Late in the year, when the bush is tinder-dry, lightning strikes are the most common cause of very hot wildfires that destroy much native habitat.

When the rains pour down in Katherine Gorge, the river level can rise more than ten metres in a few hours and floodwaters have been known to peak at the top of the escarpment.

The red bush apple ripens between October and February. It is a spectacular-looking, crisp and crunchy fruit that is usually eaten raw. The juice from cooked fruit is drunk for coughs and colds.

The MacDonnell Ranges in central Australia are doused with an ethereal red glow as the sun sets in the middle of the year. The 'Macs' are a refuge for plants and wildlife that gather around waterholes and in cool, hidden canyons.

Fire that rages through the northern woodland in the dry winter months does more good than harm – for Aboriginal people, fire cleanses the country and allows new shoots to generate, attracting game. Dry season fires do less damage than the wildfires later in the year when the land is parched and bone dry.

Clouds build up at Cobourg Peninsula at the end of the dry, when tropical storms fill the night sky with amazing electrical displays that range far out to sea.

Native grasses and sedges reach their peak in an iridescent green when Top End plains become flooded and waterlogged after a long rainy season.

A red kangaroo stands among the spinifex grass and looks out over the desert.

Silt flows out of 17-Mile Creek, near Katherine, during the first flush of the wet.

A massive storm approaches the Arnhem Land escarpment near Mt Borradaile, signalling the end of a long, dry spell. Such storms bring welcome relief to the landscape, plants and animals that have endured months without water.

# Captions

pages 32-35

Yolngu men and boys use pronged spears to catch fish in the crystal-clear waters of north-east Arnhem Land. For people attuned to hunting in shallow water, spears are far more effective than rods and reels.

Nowdays, access is far easier because of motorised boats. Coastal islands have traditionally been excellent hunting areas for saltwater people who often travelled offshore to gather turtle eggs and hunt for creatures like dugong.

Five species of saltwater turtles inhabit north Australian waters. The green turtle is one of the most common, coming ashore to breed all along the Top End coast.

The vibrantly coloured coral trout is good eating and just as popular as the barramundi and mangrove jack.

The ebb and flow of large tides in northern Australia exposes large areas at low tide. This fringe area between the low and high tides is exploited by coast dwellers.

At first glance, north Australia's mangrove forests appear harsh and forbidding, full of grey, sticky mud, decaying timber and biting insects. However, they are one of nature's most abundant larders.

Tracy Puruntatameri holds a handful of turtle eggs, looking like a collection of ping-pong balls. The eggs can be eaten raw or hard-boiled in a billy.

A clump of pandanus palms stands beside the Arafura Sea, near Cobourg Peninsula, in Arnhem Land. The brilliant sunset is typical of dry season weather in the Top End.

A painting of a dugong on the school wall at Borroloola, in the Gulf of Carpentaria, shows that the creature is an integral part of Aboriginal mythology - good eating for some clans and a totem for others.

Living among the mud and sand, coastal mangroves are great colonisers of the foreshore. Slowly, over time, they extend Australia's landmass by capturing silt and detritus that flow out during the wet season. Mangroves are outstanding nurseries for fish, crustaceans and birds.

# Captions

pages 68-71

Giant paperbark trees grow at Yellow Water in Kakadu National Park. Traditionally, Aboriginal people used these trees extensively for shelter, to make rafts for hunting waterfowl on the plains, as medicine and to wrap food, and even bodies.

Small and pretty, the agile wallaby is a popular food source, despite being difficult to catch.

The long-neck turtle is a staple food source for people who hunt in the freshwater environment. The turtles are 'eating machines' when food is abundant at the end of the wet; they then lie beneath the mud in the dry season and wait for the rains.

Lying dormant and silent, the saltwater crocodile is the top predator in northern Australia. It can explode from the water at speeds of up to 80 km/h to take its prey.

Goannas and monitors are the largest lizards in Australia. They are powerful diggers and often shelter in burrows and hollow logs. A goanna will often stand its ground when approached, arching its back and hissing.

Anbangbang billabong is an outstanding feature of Kakadu NP. At the end of a good wet season, the billabong is full of wildlife, as attested to by the beautiful rock art paintings on the walls and ceilings of nearby Nourlangie Rock (behind).

With water lily stems over one shoulder, Malcolm Wilson of Naiyu community searches Mission Hole billabong for long-neck turtles.

A tell-tale stem and small innocuous flower are the only signs of the presence of the bush potato, a healthy tuber popular in the north.

Despite the orange nuts of the cycad palm being poisonous, they were eaten by Aboriginal people after extensive preparation. The nuts were crushed or chopped into small pieces and soaked in running water for four days to leach out the toxins. The seeds were then ground into flour and baked into damper.

Black-and-white magpie geese gather in their thousands around waterholes towards the end of the dry season, but with the onset of the wet, they spread right across the Top End. Their beautiful honking call can be heard as they fly at night between billabongs.

The woody, wedge-shaped fruit of the pandanus spiralis tree can be eaten raw or roasted, and the ends of fresh fruit are sucked or chewed for juice. The plant is very important to Aboriginal people, who weave the prepared leaves into mats, dilly bags and rope.

Double-page spread: Early morning light shines on the Flora River as water flows over a build-up of limestone called a tufa dam. Remote and pristine, the Flora is a tributary of the Daly River which has fed north Australian Aboriginal people for centuries.

# Captions
pages 110-113

Waterholes such as this one at Tempe Downs, in central Australia, are refuges and sanctuaries for people and animals in the desert.

The red kangaroo is the world's largest living marsupial and has adapted well to living in arid areas. Traditionally, kangaroos were prized tucker for desert dwellers.

Witchetty grubs are found in the roots of an acacia tree known as the witchetty bush. They are the larvae of moths that burrow into and live in the roots of the bush.

Kangaroo tails are cooked in the coals. When the hide is burned or peeled away a layer of tasty, nutritious fat is exposed.

Emus were once common in the northern parts of the arid lands but their numbers have been reduced by hunting and livestock, which trample eggs and eat the emu's food.

After the rains, the central Australian desert comes alive with wild flowers such as these large pussytails. Most plants flower and seed abundantly to take advantage of the good weather.

Rippled by the wind and bearing the imprints of passing animals, this red dune in the Simpson Desert is part of the world's largest sand dune desert that was formed some 18,000 years ago. While inhospitable to people, the Simpson is home to many small animals that thrive in the hot, hostile terrain.

The bustard, or bush turkey is prized by Aboriginal people. The bird carries substantial meat but its Australia-wide range has declined by nearly 90 per cent in the past century because livestock now dominates the birds' grassland habitat. Poor bustard.

Spinifex grass is a dominant feature of the desert. Its spiky needles provide protection for many small mammals, marsupials and reptiles. After rain, the grass turns green but in the dry months, spinifex is a straw colour.

The perentie is the second-largest lizard in the world, sometimes measuring more than 2.5 metres in length. It is active in the warmer months and often lives deep in the crevices of rocky outcrops.

A golden afterglow fills the sky around Chambers Pillar, near Titjikala, south of Alice Springs. The pillar, a sandstone obelisk towering 50 metres above the desert, is an important site for Arrente people.

Spinifex sandplain typical of the south-west region of the N.T. The honey grevillea provided indigenous people wit a rare source of sugar. The tall dense shrubby trees are young desert oaks. Photo by Mike Gillam.

# Alternative Ingredients

**Bush coconut** – desiccated coconut

**Bush onions** – shallots

**Bush peach** (quandong) – stonefruit

**Bush peanuts** – peanuts, macadamias, pistachio

**Bush tomatoes** – sundried tomatoes

**Bush turkey** – stewing steak or lamb

**Crocodile** – chicken, pork

**Dugong** – chicken, pork

**Emu** – stewing steak

**Freshwater mussels** – sea, black or green-lip mussels

**Freshwater prawns** – prawns

**Freshwater turtle** – veal

**Goanna** – chicken

**Longbums** – nothing similar

**Magpie goose** – goose or duck

**Mangrove worms** – nothing similar

**Mud mussels** – sea, black or green lip mussels

**Pepper berries** – Madagascan pickled peppers, red or green

**Rye berries** – blue berries

**Sugarbag** – honey

**Turtle** – lamb, chicken, veal, fillet steak

**Turtle eggs** – nothing similar, in a dish where it is for decoration, use quail or bantam eggs

**Water lily pod seeds** – peanuts

**Water lily stems** – celery

**Wild plums** – blueberries

**Wild spinach** – English spinach

**Witchetty grubs** – nothing similar

# Where to buy Bush Tucker

**Bush Tucker Shop**
**Kurrajong Australian Native Foods**
Tel: +61 2 8883 3955
Fax: +61 2 8883 3900
E: wow@bushtuckershop.com
Web: www.bushtuckershop.com

**Outback Bushfoods**
PO Box 8283, Alice Springs NT, 0871
Tel: +61 8 9953 3354
Fax: +61 8 9953 3354
E: diliji@outbackbushfoods.com.au
Web: www.outbackbushfoods.com.au

**Outback Chef**
E: debbie@outbackchef.com.au
Web: http://stores.ebay.com.au/

**Vic Cherikoff Food Services Pty Ltd**
rear 167 Kingsgrove Rd, Kingsgrove, NSW, 2208
Tel: +61 2 9554 9477
Mob: 0418 405 183
Fax: +61 2 9554 9633
E: vic@cherikoff.net
Web: http://www.cherikoff.net/cherikoff/

**Basically Wild**
Basically Wild Edible Art, 182 Witta Rd, Maleny, Queensland, 4552
Tel: + 61 7 54 944 970
E: info@wild-foods.com
Web: www.wild-foods.com

**Ni Ni Well**
Tel/Fax: 1300 131 231
Mob: 0411 248 917
E: niniwell@optusnet.com.au

**Australian Rainforest Products Pty Ltd**
PO Box 6136, South Lismore, NSW, 2480
Tel: +61 2 6689 7414
Fax: +61 2 6689 7565
E: sibylla@australianrainforestproducts.com
Web: www.australianrainforestproducts.com

**Tumbeela Native Bushfoods**
PO Box 80, Verdun, South Australia, 5245
Tel: +61 8 8388 7360
Fax: +61 8 8388 1065
E: tumbeela@ozemail.com.au
Web: www.adelaidehillsfood.com.au/tumbeela

**Tanamera Bush Foods**
Hunt Road, McLaren Flat, South Australia, 5171
Tel: +61 8 8383 0374
Fax: +61 8 8383 0374

**Green Farmhouse**
PO Box 92, Millicent, South Australia, 5280
Tel: +61 8 8735 2043
Fax: +61 8 8735 2090
E: gfh@seol.net.au
Web: www.greenfarmhouse.com

**Arnhem Bushtucker**
PO Box 42801, Casuarina NT, 0811
Tel: +61 8 8988 4546
Fax: +61 8 8988 4534
E: we_venture@bigpond.com

**Bushfood Store**
Web: www.bushtucker.com.au

Various suppliers
Web: www.hotkey.net.au/~bushfood/

# *Postscript*

I have the good fortune to know Steve Sunk. We were colleagues for many years teaching commercial cookery at Regency Hotel School. His rapport with students of all ages and many different walks of life was evident to me very early in my career, so it is no surprise that he has had huge success with the Aboriginal people of the Northern Territory.

When he first went to Darwin with his family to take up a position teaching hospitality, his enthusiasm was contagious. As time went by he was telling me of his trips to the Daly River teaching his trade of cooking to the young. He was in his element.

His courses were not just about cooking, they were about education, confidence, self-esteem, nutrition and health. These issues are paramount in the development of the daily lives of Aboriginal people.

The recipes he has developed, using the local foods and adding ingredients from local stores, have given the students an insight into their own cuisine. Aboriginal cuisine is ancient and in the past the population did not suffer the diseases of the western world. Takeaway food, with its high fat and sugar content, has wreaked havoc on the Aboriginal population, as it has on everyone else. Nutrition is a vital element in both the management and prevention of these diseases.

By using accessible ingredients Steve has devised a means of marrying the ancient and the classical methods of cookery.

I recommend this book to every chef as a great resource for the development of their own skills and knowledge.

This book is also the beginning of a journey across cultures and food from a diverse range of communities.

Carmen Vining
Chef, Lecturer

# The **Fred Hollows** Foundation

The Fred Hollows Foundation carries on the work of the late Professor Fred Hollows (1929-1993).

Fred was an eye doctor, a skilled surgeon of international renown, a champion of the right of all people to good health and a strong advocate for social justice.

Since 1992, the foundation established in his name has helped restore the sight of well over one million people in more than 20 countries.

In Australia, The Fred Hollows Foundation works with local communities and Indigenous organisations to ensure that Indigenous Australians enjoy the same health and life expectancy as other Australians. Our current programs focus on nutrition, community stores, literacy, women's centres and building governance capacity in the Jawoyn region east of Katherine in the Northern Territory.

We also play an advocacy role on the national stage in relation to the general and eye health needs of Indigenous people, especially those living in remote regions.

Thanks to The Fred Hollows Foundation and its local partners, patients with restored sight are returning to work, doctors are passing on their new-found skills by training colleagues and Indigenous Australians are taking ownership of activities which impact their health and life expectancy.

For more information or to make a donation visit www.hollows.org or call 1800 352 352 in Australia.

**ARAFURA CATERING EQUIPMENT**

As a Northern Territory family based company, **Arafura Catering Services** is proud to be associated with Walkabout Chefs.

The Pearson family has been living in the Territory for the past 20 years and is very active in the local community.

Arafura Catering Equipment works closely with Aboriginal communities and services remote community needs including consultations for new kitchen designs and equipment.

The company is committed to the preparation of healthy food in communities, particularly through local takeaway outlets and kitchens, and encourages any initiative to achieve this goal, especially among the elderly and young children.

The Back to Basics program has given Aboriginal people the skills to combine traditional bush foods with western foods and to use different cooking techniques and tools. The program has highlighted the value of traditional foods in delivering healthy food options to community members.

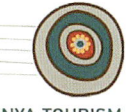

GUNYA TOURISM

Formed after nine months of negotiation with local elders, **Gunya Titjikala** is a harmonious joint venture between Gunya Tourism and the Titjikala Aboriginal Community. The joint venture is all about equality, with 50 per cent ownership in capital, profit sharing and management committee seats. The venture started operation in September 2004.

Titjikala Aboriginal Community Chairman, Phillip Wilyuka, says: "This is for the youth of our community. It's a wonderful opportunity to showcase our people, our culture, landscapes and our language to international and domestic tourists, but most importantly to do this in partnership with Gunya Tourism."

Gunya Tourism developed the Indigenous Tourism Business Model designed around allowing a remote Aboriginal community to participate in a high-yielding tourism venture which was created with private funding without any government financial assistance. It offers a pathway to economic independence providing employment, social stability and the preservation of culture and traditions.

Best of all, 50 per cent of the profits from the Gunya Titjikala resort are placed back into the Titjikala Foundation supporting health, education and school retention activities within the Titjikala community.

Visit www.gunya.com.au

*Good Food, Good Life*

Nestlé's motto of "Good Food, Good Life" is being actively applied in the Northern Territory through programs designed to improve health, nutrition, well-being and pride among the Aboriginal communities. These include:

• Regular cook-ups arranged with the Arnhem Land Progress Association to promote nutritious meal solutions at bush community stores.

• The donation of selected Nestlé products to Charles Darwin University for use in cook-ups by Aboriginal hospitality students.

• An annual donation of $30,000 to Territory Tidy Towns uniting local government, business and the community in improving the local environment and developing confidence and pride in Aboriginal communities.

• Participation with MILO and other selected Nestlé products in healthy breakfast programs being trialled in several Arnhem Land primary schools.

Nestlé's partnership with GI Ltd, the body promoting the use of Glycemic Index in conjunction with sound nutrition, is particularly relevant in the light of the health needs of Aboriginal people.

We hope that our commitment to improving the health of Aboriginal people will spark other corporations to become involved, raising the standard of health to that of the general Australian population and beyond.

167

# Acknowledgments

Steve Sunk and David Hancock would like to acknowledge and thank many people and organisations for their assistance with this book. Some of these people and organisations appear below. There are others, too numerous to list, who have helped in some way. Thanks to everyone for your support.

Vice Chancellor Professor Helen Garnett, Charles Darwin University • Professor Charles Webb, CDU • Associate Professor Martin Jarvis, Artistic Director of Darwin Symphony Orchestra • Leigh Harding, Cookery Lecturer, CDU • John Greatorex, Lecturer, Yolngu studies CDU • Roy Lockhead, Chef • Lajamanu Community and Local Government • Lajamanu Progress Association • James Butler, Operation Manager, LPA • Robyn Butler, Lajamanu Store Manager • Lynette Tasman, President, Lajamanu Community • Lajamanu CEC and Teachers • Laramba Community and Local Council • Laramba Community Women's Centre • Alison Mcklay, Nutrition Coordinator, Centre Region • Gunya Tourism • Bill Moss, AM, Group Head, Macquarie Bank, Banking and Property Group • Beverly Baker, Community Liaison Manager, Macquarie Bank • Titjikala Community and Local Council • Titjikala Community Women's Centre • Phillip Willyuka, Chairman, Titjikala Council • Harry Scott, CEO, Titjikala Council • Nestle Food Services • Greg Smith, Area Manager NT, NFS • Sherril Page, National Marketing Manager, NFS • Roger Pearson, Managing Director, Arafura Catering Equipment • Galiwinku Community and Local Government • Peter Moore, Principal, Sheperdson CEC • Ian Gumbula, CDEP Co-ordinator, Galiwinku • Galiwinku Women's Health • Wadeye (Port Keats) Community and Local Council • Jolene Killer, Tenille Skinner and Vanita Skeen, Luma Luma Community, WA • Emma Connellan and senior girls, OLSH THANMERRURR • Jan Pilcher-Juniper, Principal, OLSH School • Tobias Naganbe, Principal, OLSH School • Theodora Narndu, Elder, story woman • Daly River Community and Local Council • Miriam Rose Bauman, Principal, Xavier School, Senior elder • Barak Sam Bono • Ronald Cooper • Beatrice Wombtjy • Bridget Kikitin • Katherine Arrina • Timber Creek Community • Timber Creek Women's Centre • Philip Gigante • Daguragu Community • Tiwi Island Communities • Norm Buchan CEO, Tiwi Island Training and Employment • Dr William Griffiths, Director, Catholic Education, Diocese of Darwin • Northern Territory Education Department • Carmen Vining • Zonta Club SA • Greg Corbet, NT Manager, 3M Australia Pty Ltd • Clara Tusim • Margaret Sunk • Jess Sunk.

Professor David Bowman, School of Environmental Research, CDU • Greg Miles • Hyacinth Tungatalum • Tony Pilakui • Tim Palipuaminni • Joseph Puantulura • Simon Kalpa • Peter Yates and Jock Morse , Outback Bush Foods • Glenn Wightman, NT Parks and Wildlife Commission • Jacko Angeles, Menzies School of Health • Jennifer Koenig Price, Northern Land Council • Francine Chinn • Jane Hodson, Central Land Council • Bill Harney and his mob • Karlu Karlu ladies • Davenport Ranges mob • Iain Summers • Dylan Walters • Michael Silver • Peter and Sheila Forrest • Bevil Staley • Kieran Finnane • Jackie Chlanda • Erwin Chlanda • Averil Moffat, Australian Geographic • Vere Kenny, AUSCAPE • Mike Gillam • Jean-Paul Ferrero • Chris and Lynne Bramhill • Rosemary Hancock • Helen Hancock • Arthur Hancock • Denise Kenney • Tony Morison • Ian Morris: Natural History Guide to Kakadu • Peter Latz: Bushfires and Bushtucker • John Brock: Native Plants of Northern Australia • Semko • Brooke Hancock • Ward Hancock.

The publishers would like to offer special thanks to the organisations appearing on the previous pages for their generous support and belief in this project.